Briefly:
John Stuart Mill's *On Liberty*

Briefly:
John Stuart Mill's
On Liberty

David Mills Daniel

scm press

The Author has asserted his right under the Copyright, Designs and
Patents Act, 1988, to be identified as the Author of this Work

The author and publisher acknowledge material reproduced from John
Stuart Mill, *On Liberty and Other Essays*, ed. J. Gray, 1998, Oxford and
New York: Oxford University Press, ISBN 0192833847. Reprinted by
permission of Oxford Universiy Press. All rights reserved.

British Library Cataloguing in Publication data

A catalogue record for this book is available
from the British Library

0 334 04036 1/978 0 334 04036 1

First published in 2006 by SCM Press
9–17 St Alban's Place,
London N1 0NX

www.scm-canterburypress.co.uk

SCM Press is a division of
SCM-Canterbury Press Ltd

Printed and bound in Great Britain by
Bookmarque, Croydon, Surrey

Contents

Introduction

The SCM *Briefly* series is designed to enable students and general readers to acquire knowledge and understanding of key texts in philosophy, philosophy of religion, theology and ethics. While the series will be especially helpful to those following university and A-level courses in philosophy, ethics and religious studies, it will in fact be of interest to anyone looking for a short guide to the ideas of a particular philosopher or theologian.

Each book in the series takes a piece of work by one philosopher and provides a summary of the original text, which adheres closely to it, and contains direct quotations from it, thus enabling the reader to follow each development in the philosopher's argument(s). Throughout the summary, there are page references to the original philosophical writing, so that the reader has ready access to the primary text. In the Introduction to each book, you will find details of the edition of the philosophical work referred to.

In *Briefly: Mill's On Liberty*, we refer to John Stuart Mill, *On Liberty and Other Essays*, edited by John Gray, 1998, Oxford and New York: Oxford University Press, ISBN 0192833847.

Each *Briefly* begins with an Introduction, followed by a chapter on the Context in which the work was written. Who was this writer? Why was this book written? With Some Issues to Consider, and some Suggested Further Reading,

Introduction

this *Briefly* aims to get anyone started in their philosophical investigation. The detailed summary of the philosophical work is followed by a concise chapter-by-chapter overview and an extensive glossary of terms.

Bold type is used in the Detailed Summary and Overview sections to indicate the first occurrence of words and phrases that appear in the Glossary. The Glossary also contains terms used elsewhere in this *Briefly* guide and other terms that readers may encounter in their study of Mill's *On Liberty*.

Context

Who was John Stuart Mill?

John Stuart Mill was born in London in 1806, and was the son of James Mill, the utilitarian philosopher and friend of Jeremy Bentham, the founder of utilitarianism. The education that Mill received from his father, and which he describes in his *Autobiography*, was unusually ambitious. He started Greek and Latin when he was a few years old, lacked friends of his own age, and did not take part in sport; and this intense programme may have contributed to the severe depression he suffered when he was about 20. In 1823, Mill joined the East India Company, which at that time governed India, where he worked until the British government took over responsibility for India in 1858. During this time, Mill was developing, and writing about, his views on philosophical and political issues, and working out his own version of utilitarianism. *On Liberty* (1859), *Utilitarianism* (1861), *Considerations on Representative Government* (1861) and *The Subjection of Women* (1869) have had a major and continuing influence on moral and political philosophy, as well as on thinking about the rights of individuals and minorities, and the relationship between the individual and the state. Mill married Mrs Harriet Taylor, whom he had known for more than 20 years, in 1851, and was Liberal MP for Westminster between 1865 and 1868. He died in France in 1873.

What is *On Liberty*?

The question that Mill addresses in *On Liberty* affects people to a much greater extent today than in 1859, when it was published. How much power is society entitled to exercise over the individual? Mill recognized that these questions had assumed greater, not less, significance, as, during the nineteenth century, reform movements and revolutions led to the establishment of more democratic governments. In a non-democratic state, such as the monarchies that had governed most European countries in the eighteenth century, it was clear that rulers and ruled had different interests. Those who opposed such governments sought to replace them with elected ones, chosen by and responsible to the majority of the people, which would look after their interests and thus eliminate conflict between rulers and ruled. Mill, however, thought it naive to think that the arrival of democracy would solve all problems. On the contrary, the rise of elected governments meant that the issue of individual freedom tended to be overlooked.

A democratic government represents the majority, but what about individuals and minorities who have not chosen that particular government, whom it does not represent, and to whom it might be hostile, or those minorities or individuals whose opinions are at odds with the majority in society? It is necessary to safeguard their rights against the tyranny of the majority. And (Mill argues) such tyranny does not necessarily take the form of political oppression by government itself. It may be social tyranny, involving the use of public opinion to coerce nonconformists into acceptance of majority views and modes of behaviour.

So, where should the boundary between individual freedom and society's legitimate interference with individual conduct be drawn? Mill proposes what he calls 'one very simple principle' to regulate society's control over the individual: that the only purpose for which society may exercise power over one of its members, against his will, is where his conduct may harm others or their interests. In matters affecting only himself or his interests, the individual (children and those incapable of managing their affairs being excepted) must have absolute independence.

Of course, this principle of individual liberty is less simple to apply than to state. Opinions will vary as to whether or not certain actions harm others, or, even if this is agreed, whether or not they should be banned or tolerated. But Mill's point is that, unless there are compelling reasons to the contrary, and the behaviour in question is clearly harming others or their interests, individual freedom should always be preferred to social control. As Mill explains, a range of historical, religious, cultural and social factors determine the values of a particular society, from religious beliefs, through the interests of a particular social class, to a society's 'likings and dislikings'. However much importance it places on its values, society, or the majority in it, should not impose them on dissentient individuals and minorities, and thus restrict their freedom, unless their actions involve harm to others.

For example, until after the middle of the twentieth century, society in Britain disapproved of homosexuality, and homosexual relationships were against the law, even though what took place between two consenting adults could not harm others or their interests. Today, in Britain, fox-hunting is banned, even though it is hard to see how those who pursue this minority sport can cause harm to others. Of course, it is true that many people had or have strong moral or religious objections to both. But would either the former ban on

3

homosexual relationships, or the current ban on fox-hunting, pass the test of Mill's very simple principle? Were, or are, the restrictions on personal liberty they involve justified by the standard he proposes?

Mill maintains that all matters relating to conscience and the expression and publication of opinion, including press freedom, fall within the 'region of human liberty', and no restrictions should be placed on them. This is consistent with his principle of individual liberty, but he argues that, quite apart from the matter of individual freedom, there are practical reasons why censorship harms society, including those in it who disagree with certain opinions, and want to suppress them. Most human opinions and conduct are rational because they can be corrected through discussion. Indeed, truth is usually arrived at through a combining and reconciling of opposite points of view. For this to be possible, people need to be able hear a wide range of different points of view on a subject and, even when an opinion has become the majority one, it should continue to be scrutinized and debated. A suppressed opinion on a particular matter may be the true one, or it may contain an important (but neglected) part of the truth, which the generally accepted opinion lacks. Mill uses the example of Christian morality. Some claim that it provides a complete system of morality, but (in his view) it needs to be supplemented by Greek and Roman morality, with their greater emphasis on the ideas of duty and public obligation. Further, even if the majority opinion is true, unless it is challenged it will be held as a mere dogma, not a belief that has 'living power'. He considers that this had happened to Christianity. It was no longer a dynamic, growing religion because its beliefs and values were generally accepted, so its followers no longer had to defend them against challenge and criticism.

In a democratic society, few would challenge Mill's argument for freedom of expression. But can it always be the paramount consideration, or are there occasions when, even in a democratic society, it needs to be curbed, because the views being expressed may lead to incitement of hatred against individuals or groups, or even be directed at destruction of the democratic society itself? As Mill acknowledges, it is one thing to denounce corn-dealers as starvers of the poor in the press, but another to do so to an excited mob, in front of a corn-dealer's house.

Mill has little patience with the view that the proponents of controversial or minority opinions should express them with restraint, to minimize offence, and even less with any suggestion that there should be legislation to regulate the matter. People with strong views often express them with a passion that opponents find objectionable, but this is in the nature of public debate. What he does deplore is any attempt, particularly by the supporters of the majority view, to represent their opponents as bad or immoral, simply because of their views, which can deter them from making their case. Mill's insistence on mutual fairness and tolerance in public debate seems particularly relevant today, when, in the political world, 'spin', misrepresentation of opponents' views and assaults on their integrity have become commonplace.

But individual freedom is not just about people's views and how they are expressed; it is also about how they lead their lives. Although Mill accepts that actions, where the potential for harm to others is greater, cannot be as free as opinions, he felt that nineteenth-century European society, which was increasingly dominated by mass public opinion, as reflected in mass circulation newspapers, discouraged individuality and originality, thus impoverishing human life. Afraid to be different, people were too ready to let society decide how they should live, rather than choosing for themselves. The consequence was that many people were unable to achieve their full potential, and lead fulfilled and happy lives, because they felt compelled to conform to the approved standard of conduct, while society was denied the benefit of the new ideas that unconventional lifestyle choices might generate, as these only occur in conditions of freedom and individuality.

Mill maintains that, with democratic governments increasingly pandering to the demands of the masses that elected them, the general trend in society was towards acceptance of the 'despotism of custom', making progress difficult. He makes a plea for the cultivation of individuality. Society needs eccentrics, who will flout mass opinion, and live unconventional lives, and whose value lies less in their being right than in their refusal to bend the knee to custom, which sets an example to others.

It could be argued that Mill adopts too extreme a position here. While individuals often lead the way in political and social reform, his view that all wise and noble things come from individuals, and that no democratic government can rise above the level of the mediocre seems exaggerated and elitist. It was proved wrong by, for example, the important reforms introduced by William Gladstone's 1868–74 Liberal government which, following the 1867 Reform Act, was elected on a much more democratic franchise than its predecessors. But Mill is also pointing out a danger that democratic governments face. They are elected by the people, and must represent their interests, but this does not mean they should allow their voters to do their thinking for them. They must provide leadership, not follow the dictates of public opinion. Mill also makes the perceptive point that the rule of custom, although it impedes progress, does not necessarily rule out change, provided the change applies to, or is accepted by, everyone. So a proposed reform may be resisted, but once it is introduced, it immediately becomes the new orthodoxy, which everyone must accept. Any continuing opponents of the reform will be regarded as being as eccentric as its proponents were previously.

In Chapter IV of *On Liberty*, Mill explores the question of where the boundary between what he calls 'self-regarding' actions (those that affect only the individual) and actions that affect others (with which society is entitled to interfere) should be drawn. Society is entitled to punish those who harm others, whether by law or public opinion, but, although it may encourage people to cultivate self-regarding virtues, point out their mistakes to them, and, if they do not change their ways, shun them, it is not entitled to interfere with conduct, however foolish, that affects only the individual himself. The evil of compelling an individual to act against his wishes, even for his own good, is greater than the mistakes (and their consequences), which follow from his choosing for himself.

However, in practice, is there such a thing as a purely self-regarding action? Smoking seems to be one. If an individual chooses to smoke, despite the risks involved, he is the one who will have to face the consequences. But do the consequences affect only the smoker? At home or in a public place, his smoking will make conditions unpleasant for other people. If he becomes ill, it will cause distress to family and friends. Treating the illnesses that result from smoking imposes costs on the health service; and so on.

Mill uses the example of drinking. In itself, drinking alcohol is a self-regarding action, but it ceases to be one if a heavy drinker is unable, because of it, to look after a family or meet financial obligations. Then society is entitled at least to express its disapproval. But he warns against society interfering with purely personal conduct, just to impose the majority view of what is good on a minority, as he thought was the case in some parts of the United States, where the sale of alcohol was banned. However the example of alcohol just illustrates the practical difficulties of distinguishing between purely self-regarding actions and those that affect others. Mill is severe on the temperance movements, in Britain as well as the United States, as examples of organizations wanting to impose their view of what is good on others. But when people drink alcohol outside their own homes, it is not a purely personal act. It does have a public dimension, because it can and does affect others. Banning it would be an extreme measure, but few people would want alcohol consumption to be free of regulation by society: not so that the majority can impose their view of what is good on the minority, but to protect the rest of society from inconvenience and harm.

Again, if we applied Mill's argument, would we have to regard the taking (as opposed to the selling) of drugs as a self-regarding action, with which society should not interfere? After all, our present anti-drug laws control individual conduct for the individual's own good, as well as to prevent harm to others. Mill himself acknowledges that it is legitimate for governments to restrict the sale of alcohol to prevent breaches of the peace, while the sellers' interest in promoting consumption for purposes of profit justifies regulation of its sale. He also accepts that, while taxation of alcohol simply to reduce consumption is illegitimate interference with individual liberty, taxation of what is a non-essential item for revenue-raising purposes is not.

If society, in the interests of individual freedom, must tolerate actions of which it disapproves, does it have to tolerate the activities of those who, perhaps for personal profit, encourage others to commit such actions? Mill concedes that, while society must tolerate fornication and gambling, it is more difficult to decide whether it must also tolerate pimps and casino owners.

Mill considers that, in nineteenth-century British society, there were instances of liberty being allowed where it should be denied and vice-versa. Husbands were permitted despotic and unacceptable powers over their wives, as were parents over their children. Yet, the state did not, as he thought it should (and began to through the Elementary Education Acts from 1870 onwards), compel parents to ensure that their children received an education. In fact, Mill was opposed to the state providing education, except as one type of educational provision among many, fearing that it would become a means of moulding children to be exactly the same, and thus of preventing the development of individuality. However, he held that the state should provide public examinations, to assess children's progress and check if parents were carrying out their responsibilities. Interestingly and perhaps surprisingly, Mill thought it would be legitimate for the state to pass laws preventing couples from marrying, unless they could prove the means of supporting children, in order to prevent children being brought up in conditions of extreme poverty and wretchedness.

To what extent is it acceptable for the state to help its citizens, rather than leaving them to fend for themselves? Overall, Mill is opposed to too much assistance, because it would lead to what we might call 'big government'. Generally, people do things better, and become more responsible and self-reliant citizens, if left to themselves, while any increase in government activity simply adds to its power, including its power over individuals, which is undesirable. He was afraid that if the state began to take over the role of free institutions, such as banks, insurance companies, universities, local councils and voluntary organizations, neither a free press nor a democratic constitution could ensure the country remained a free one. As central government accumulated power and administrative functions, the state bureaucracy (civil service) would expand, so that in the end, the most able people would be state employees, while the rest would become dependent upon it, and thus its docile instruments, incapable of individual initiative. Mill urges that, as far as possible, administrative functions should be given to local authorities, with central government's role confined to supervision and the dissemination of information. It is interesting to speculate on what Mill would think of the massive expansion of government activity that has taken place since his day.

Perhaps, every politician, political activist and political campaigner should keep *On Liberty* to hand. It does not provide a simple means of determining the extent to which the state or society is entitled to restrict individual liberty. But Mill's principle of individual liberty affirms that ensuring individual liberty must be a priority, and that the state or society should only restrict it if there are compelling reasons for doing so. Mill also makes the important points that: in itself, democracy is no guarantee of individual liberty and democratic governments can be too ready to pander to their electorates; for opinions and decisions to be soundly based, all points of view on a subject need to be freely expressed and listened to with respect; the majority opinion may be wrong, and minority or individual opinion right; and the over-expansion of state power and functions can restrict individual liberty and inhibit development of responsible and self-reliant citizens.

Some Issues to Consider

- Mill believed that individual and minority rights need protection in a democratic society, because the majority, whether by political oppression or the tyranny of public opinion, may seek to impose its views on individuals and minorities.

- Mill proposed that his principle of individual liberty should regulate society's control over the individual: the only purpose for which society may control the individual is to prevent harm to others or their interests.

- Mill maintained that all matters relating to conscience and the expression and publication of opinion, including press freedom, fall within the region of individual freedom, and should not be restricted.

- He thought that censorship harms society, not only by limiting freedom, but because a banned opinion may be true or contain some truth, or will challenge the accepted one and prevent it becoming a mere dogma.

- Can a democratic society always make freedom of expression its paramount consideration, or are there some opinions it is entitled to prevent being expressed?

- Mill urged those who engage in public debate to treat their opponents with respect, and not to misrepresent their views or attack their integrity.

- Mill feared that people were too ready to have their views and way of life dictated to them by public opinion, and believed there should be more emphasis on individuality, which would encourage people to choose their way of life for themselves.

- Was Mill right to think that all good and wise things come from individuals?

- Do democratic governments tend to pander to their electorates, rather than providing leadership?
- Mill defines a self-regarding action as one that affects only the individual. But is there really such a thing as a purely self-regarding action? And, even if there is, does this mean that society should not intervene to stop people doing things, which (it judges) will cause them harm?
- Mill was opposed to state-provided education, because he feared it would become a means by which the state moulds people to become exactly the same, so preventing development of individuality.
- Mill believed that, in general, people do things better, and become more responsible and self-reliant citizens, if they are left to do things for themselves.
- Was Mill right to fear that expansion of state power and functions and an increase in the size of the state bureaucracy (civil service) would threaten individual freedom?

Suggestions for Further Reading

John Stuart Mill, *On Liberty and Other Essays*, ed. J. Gray, 1998, Oxford and New York: Oxford University Press.

John Stuart Mill, *Utilitarianism*, ed. G. Sher, second edition, 2001, Indianapolis/Cambridge: Hackett Publishing Company.

John Stuart Mill, *Autobiography*, ed. J. M. Robson, 1989, London: Penguin.

N. Capaldi, 2004, *John Stuart Mill: A Biography*, Cambridge: Cambridge University Press.

J. Gray and G. W. Smith (eds), 1991, *John Stuart Mill's On Liberty in Focus*, London: Routledge.

Suggestions for Further Reading

J. Riley, 1998, *Routledge Philosophy Guidebook to Mill on Liberty*, London: Routledge.

W. Thomas, 1985, *John Stuart Mill*, Oxford and New York: Oxford University Press.

Detailed Summary of John Stuart Mill's
On Liberty

Chapter I (pp. 5–19)

Introductory

The subject of this essay is not the '**Liberty of the Will**', but '**Civil or Social Liberty**': the 'nature and limits' of the power which society can legitimately exercise over the individual (p. 5). Recent social changes make it urgent to address this rarely discussed, but divisive, question.

The 'struggle between Liberty and Authority' is one with which study of the history of Greece, Rome and **England** makes us familiar (pp. 5–6). However, in the past, it took place between governments and their subjects, with the latter seeking 'protection against the tyranny' of the former (p. 6). Generally, the position of a country's rulers was seen as 'antagonistic' to that of its subjects (p. 6). To protect the weak against the strong, it was necessary to have 'an animal of prey stronger than the rest', but, as rulers also preyed on the weak, '**patriots**' sought to limit their powers (p. 6). One way of doing this was to obtain '**political rights**', infringement of which would justify 'rebellion'; another, the creation of '**constitutional checks**', so that government acts required the '**consent**' of a **representative body** (p. 6). Most European rulers were eventually 'compelled' to concede the first 'limitation' of their power, but the second has proved harder to achieve (p. 6).

However, a time came when it ceased to seem inevitable that the interests of ruler and ruled should be opposed; the best protection against abuse of power would be to have **elected governments** (p. 6). This became the objective of 'popular' parties, and, as the 'struggle proceeded', the view gained ground, particularly within '**European liberalism**', that there would be no need to limit the powers of such governments (p. 7). As they exercised 'the nation's own power', they could be trusted not to abuse it (p. 7).

However, success reveals problems that failure might have concealed. The establishment of 'elective and responsible' governments showed that 'such phrases as "**self-government**", and "the power of the people over themselves", do not express the true state of the case' (p. 8). Rulers and ruled are not 'always the same people', while the 'will of the people' is that of its 'most numerous' or 'most active *part*' (p. 8). It became clear that it is important to limit the powers of '**accountable**' governments over individuals, and to establish safeguards against the '"**tyranny of the majority**"' (p. 8).

Such tyranny is still generally held to operate through governments, but, when 'society is itself the tyrant', it often takes the form of '**social tyranny**' (p. 8). This can be worse than '**political oppression**', because 'prevailing opinion' penetrates so 'deeply into the details of life' (pp. 8–9). Protection is needed against society's tendency to impose 'its own ideas and practices' on those who do not share them (p. 9). It is as important to set (and maintain) limits to 'the legitimate interference of **collective opinion** with **individual independence**' as it is to resist 'political **despotism**' (p. 9).

But, although the enforcement of 'restraints' on others' actions is what makes existence 'valuable', there is still (apart from a few obvious cases) a lot of work to be done on the question of where to set these restraints (p. 9). No two periods of history have 'decided it alike', but 'the magical influence of **custom**' has prevented doubt about the rules of conduct which have been adopted (p. 9). As people have been encouraged to regard their feelings as the best guide on this issue, they believe that others should be required to act as they 'would like them to' (p. 10). And, for the 'ordinary man', there is no better justification for his 'notions of **morality**, taste or **propriety**' than that they are his own preferences (p. 10). Indeed, this is his 'chief guide' in most matters, including interpretation of his '**religious creed**' (p. 10). Of course, if there is an '**ascendant class**', a large part of a country's morality comes from its '**class interests**' (pp. 10–11). Other factors determining acceptance of rules of conduct are the 'supposed preferences or aversions' of rulers or gods, or the interests of society (p. 11).

However, the rules of conduct a society adopts often have more to do with its 'likings and dislikings' than anything else. And those with new ideas are usually more concerned with ensuring their general acceptance than with defending freedom, or addressing the issue of whether or not what society prefers 'should be a law to individuals' (p. 11). The only exception has been in religion. Although most of the opponents of the Roman Catholic Church were also intolerant of religious differences, in situations where it was clear that no one religious group was going to be dominant, it was recognized that there would have to be agreement to differ. So, it is in relation to religion that the 'rights of the individual' have been asserted on 'grounds of principle'; and it is claimed that no one is accountable to others for his religious beliefs (p. 12).

However, in practice, full religious freedom is only found where there is 'religious indifference'; even in countries where there is **toleration**, most genuinely religious people have reservations about it (p. 12).

England differs from most continental countries: while the 'yoke of opinion' may be heavier, 'that of law is lighter' (p. 12). This is not so much due to respect for individual independence as to the view that the government and public have 'opposite' interests (p. 13). However, attitudes in England could change if people come to regard the government as representing their opinions and interests. Further, opposition to government 'interference' is indiscriminate, because there is no 'recognized principle' for testing its 'propriety or impropriety' (p. 13).

The 'object of this Essay' is to propose 'one very simple principle', by which to regulate society's 'dealings' with individuals, whether through the law or 'the moral coercion of public opinion' (pp. 13–14). It is that, 'the only purpose for which power can be rightfully exercised over any member of a civilized community, against his will, is to prevent harm to others' (p. 14). His own good, whether physical or moral, is not a 'sufficient warrant' (p. 14). While there may be good reasons for trying to persuade people into, or out of, actions that may cause good or harm to themselves, there is no justification for coercion or punishment. In conduct which affects only himself, the individual's 'independence is, of right, absolute'; he is only accountable to society for conduct 'which concerns others' (p. 14). Of course, there are exceptions, such as children, those who need the care of others, and 'backward states of society' (p. 14). The **principle of liberty** does not apply where people are incapable of improvement by 'free and equal discussion' (p. 14) 'Despotism' is an acceptable form of government for '**barbarians**', provided it is aimed at their improvement (pp. 14–15).

This argument for individual freedom is not based on any '**idea of abstract right**' (p. 15). **The 'ultimate appeal' in ethical matters is 'utility'**; but it must be 'grounded on the permanent interests of man as a progressive being' (p. 15). These interests permit '**external control**' of the individual only in relation to actions that affect others' interests (p. 15). However, there are social duties which individuals should be required to perform, such as giving evidence in court or defending the country: a person may do harm by his inaction as well as his actions.

The 'appropriate region of human liberty' consists of 'the inward domain of consciousness', covering **freedom of conscience**, thought, feeling and opinion on all matters, including moral and **theological** ones (p. 16). Expressing or publishing opinions seems to be in a different category, because it concerns others, but it is 'practically inseparable' from freedom of thought (pp. 16–17). We must be free to pursue our own way of life, even if others disapprove of it, provided it does not harm them. Also, with the same proviso, people must be free to join with others for any purpose. A society which lacks these liberties is not free. The only worthwhile freedom is that of pursuing our own good in whichever way we choose.

This **doctrine** may not be new, but it goes against the tendency of 'existing opinion and practice' (p. 17). The '**engines of moral repression**' are used more energetically to prevent divergences from prevailing opinion in '**self-regarding**' than in 'social matters' (p. 18). Religion has been one of the most important factors in shaping moral opinion, and religious leaders have usually wished to control 'every department of human conduct'; but so, too, do many modern reformers, such as 'M. **Comte**', even though they are no friends of religion

(p. 18). Further, the trend of both public opinion and legislation is to 'strengthen society' at the expense of individual freedom (p. 18). Indeed, people's desire to 'impose their own opinions' on others is kept in check only by their inability to do so (p. 18).

It will be convenient to consider one aspect of freedom: '**Liberty of Thought**', from which freedom of speaking and writing cannot be separated (p. 19). Of course, these freedoms are part of the '**political morality**' of all countries that 'profess religious toleration and free institutions' (p. 19). However, the 'philosophical and practical' grounds on which they rest are not as well understood as might be thought (p. 19).

Chapter II (pp. 20–61)

Of the Liberty of Thought and Discussion

It is to be hoped that no arguments are necessary in defence of **press freedom**, or against governments prescribing the opinions which people should hear. In England, although the laws in relation to the press remain 'servile', there is little danger of their being enforced; indeed, in '**constitutional** countries' generally, there is little likelihood of governments trying to control the press, except where such action reflects the 'intolerance of the public' (pp. 20–1). But such 'coercion' is 'illegitimate', even when it is in line with 'public opinion' (p. 21). If only one person held a 'contrary opinion' to everybody else, this majority would be no more entitled to silence 'that one person' than he would be to silence the majority (p. 21). An opinion is not a mere 'personal possession' (p. 21) To prevent its expression is to rob 'the human race': future generations as well as the present one, and those who disagree with it as well as those who agree (p. 21). If the opinion is right, they are unable to exchange 'error for truth'; if it is wrong, they are denied the opportunity of having the truth of their view confirmed by its 'collision with error' (p. 21).

Those who wish to suppress an opinion are not '**infallible**' (p. 22). They confuse '*their* certainty' with '*absolute* certainty' (p. 22). Sadly, while everyone recognizes their fallibility, few 'take any precautions' against it, or admit that a particular opinion they hold might be wrong (p. 22). Even those accustomed to having their opinions challenged place 'unbounded reliance' on the opinions they share with other members of their political party, religious denomination or social class (p. 22). And this attitude is not affected by the knowledge that other groups hold, or previous generations have held, different opinions. People insist on the rightness of the opinions of their particular 'world' against 'the dissentient worlds of other people' (p. 23).

It is argued that preventing the 'propagation of error' does not involve a greater 'assumption of infallibility' than any other act 'done by public authority' (p. 23). Governments and individuals should reach the 'truest opinions they can', and should not 'impose' them on others, unless they are sure of their correctness (p. 23). But they would be wrong to allow the circulation of views they believe to be 'dangerous to the welfare of mankind', just because, in the past, people have been persecuted for expressing what are now accepted as true opinions (p. 23). Governments make mistakes in all sorts of areas, but the possibility of error does not mean that they should not levy taxes or declare war.

But this will not do. There is a big difference between accepting an opinion as true, because it has not been refuted, and 'assuming its truth for the purpose of not permitting its refutation' (p. 24). Indeed, it is the possibility of having our opinions contradicted or disproved that 'justifies' our assuming their truth for 'purposes of action' (p. 24). Why is it that, on the whole, most human opinions and conduct are **'rational'** (p. 24)? It is because human beings are able to correct their mistakes through 'discussion and experience' (p. 25). The only way that human beings can approach complete knowledge of a subject 'is by hearing what can be said about it by persons of every variety of opinion' (p. 25). Only when we have defended our opinions against every possible objection are we entitled to consider them better than those 'who have not gone through a similar process' (p. 25). The only 'safeguard' of the beliefs in which we place most confidence is 'a standing invitation to the whole world to prove them unfounded' (p. 26).

It seems strange that people should acknowledge the need for free discussion, but only on *'doubtful'* subjects (p. 26). To hold an opinion as certain, while not allowing those who wish to challenge it to do so, is to make ourselves 'the judges of certainty' (p. 26). These days, people are not so much sure of their opinions as sure that they would be lost without them. Some beliefs are thought to be so important and useful to society that governments, supported by 'the general opinion of mankind', are asked not to allow them to be questioned (p. 27). However, the issue of an opinion's usefulness is itself a matter of opinion, while its truth is 'part of its utility' (p. 27). And can any untrue belief be 'really useful' (p. 27)?

But let us consider the 'concrete' example of opinions about the existence God (p. 28). People might ask whether I am arguing that it is 'assuming infallibility' to be sure of God's existence (p. 28). No: but deciding the matter *'for others'*, without allowing them to hear any opposing arguments, is (p. 28). And it makes no difference how much public support there is for banning expression of these opposing views. We should remember the case of **Socrates**. We now regard him as one of 'the most virtuous' of men, but he was put to death for 'impiety and immorality', because he denied the existence of 'the gods recognized by the State' (p. 29). What about **Jesus**, who was executed as 'a **blasphemer**' (p. 30)? Indeed, his contemporaries mistook him for 'the exact contrary of what he was' (p. 30). And those who condemned him were not 'bad men' (p. 30). Rather, they represented all 'the religious, moral and patriotic feelings of their time', and were just as sincere in their beliefs as 'respectable and pious' people today (p. 30). '**Orthodox Christians**', who think that they would have acted differently, should remember that St Paul was a leading persecutor of the early Christians (p. 30).

The example of the Emperor **Marcus Aurelius**, one of the most 'enlightened' rulers in history, also illustrates my point (p. 30). In character, he was a 'better Christian' than many so-called 'Christian sovereigns' (p. 31). However, he 'persecuted Christianity', because he thought that this new religion would undermine existing religious beliefs, which were holding society together (p. 31). We need to recognize that there is no contemporary Christian more convinced of the social dangers of **atheism** than Marcus Aurelius was of those of Christianity. Of course, we might follow Dr **Johnson**, and claim that persecution is an 'ordeal through which truth ought to pass' (p. 32). But it is not acceptable to reward the discoverers of 'new truths' with 'martyrdom' (pp. 32–3). Further, it is simply not the case that 'truth always triumphs over persecution' (p. 33). Christianity prevailed in the **Roman Empire** only because persecution was intermittent. In general, persecution always triumphs, unless 'the heretics' are too strong to be persecuted successfully (p. 33–4).

Of course, we no longer kill those who put forward 'new opinions' (p. 34). But, in England, those who express certain 'theological' beliefs can still be prosecuted, or denied justice, because of the 'legal doctrine' that only those who 'profess belief in a God' and a **future life** can give evidence in court (p. 35). So, on the basis that atheists must be liars, we accept the evidence of atheists who are willing to lie, but reject that of those brave enough to acknowledge their atheism openly. Now, this legal penalty may just be one of the 'rags and remnants of persecution', but there is always the danger, as in a 'revival of religion', that active persecution will be resumed (p. 36). Indeed, the main problem of such legal penalties is that they reinforce the 'social stigma', which (in England, particularly) attaches to, and inhibits, expression of unorthodox views (p. 37). This 'social intolerance' may prevent unwelcome challenges to accepted opinions, but, by making people hide their true beliefs, it results in the loss of 'the entire moral courage of the human mind' (pp. 37–8).

It is impossible to calculate the damage being done to people's 'mental development' by the prevention of 'fair and thorough discussion' of different points of view, even if they are erroneous ones (pp. 38–9). Freedom of thought does not allow only potentially 'great thinkers' to pursue new ideas (p. 39). It also allows 'average human beings' to become 'intellectually active people' (p. 39). If we think about it, we can see that most of the important intellectual and institutional developments in recent European history have taken place during such periods as the **Reformation**, when 'the yoke of authority was broken' (p. 40).

And, even if the 'received' opinion being challenged is true, unless it is questioned, it will be held, not as 'a living truth', but as 'a dead **dogma**' (p. 40). This is not the way that a 'truth ought to be held by a rational being', because it becomes just one more 'superstition' (p. 41). Further, if the human intellect is to be 'cultivated', this is best done through consideration of subjects on which correct beliefs are 'of the first importance', and which we ought to be able to defend in debate (p. 41). It is no argument to say that people can simply be taught 'the grounds of their opinions', because they need to understand them (p. 41). In subjects such as religion and morals, most of the arguments for a particular 'disputed opinion' are arguments against an alternative (p. 42). To know only one's own side of an argument is to know 'little of that' (p. 42). And we need to hear the opposing arguments from those who believe in them, and who will argue the case for them with conviction. It is essential to have 'opponents of all important truths'; if they do not exist, they must be imagined (p. 43).

An opponent of 'free discussion' may contend that it is sufficient for '**philosophers** and **theologians**' to understand all the arguments for and against a particular opinion; 'common men' do not need to do so, because they can rely on the 'authority' of those 'specially trained to the task' (p. 43). But this approach accepts the need for some kind of 'rational assurance' that the response to any objections is satisfactory (p. 43). However, there can be no such assurance, if objectors are denied a hearing. Without discussion, not only are the grounds of an opinion forgotten, so, too, is its meaning; a 'living belief' is replaced by its 'shell and husk' (p. 45).

The 'experience of almost all ethical doctrines and religious creeds' bears this out (p. 45). Their meaning remains 'undiminished' while the battle is on to ensure their adoption (p. 45). But, once accepted, or at least tolerated, interest in them fades; their followers cease to listen to counter arguments, or to 'trouble dissentients' with their own (p. 45). And, if a creed becomes merely 'hereditary', its 'living power' declines (pp. 45–6). Untested by 'personal experience', it ceases to connect with 'the inner life of the human being', although it acts as an obstacle to the reception of new intellectual 'influences' (p. 46).

This is how so many of its adherents treat 'the doctrines of Christianity': the 'maxims and precepts' of the **New Testament** (p. 46). Christians profess belief in such teachings as 'they should judge not, lest they be judged', and that they 'should sell all that they have and give it to the poor'; but few of them base their lives on these teachings (p. 47). Instead, they prefer to follow 'everyday' moral precepts, which, at best, only partially reflect New Testament teachings, and sometimes contradict them (p. 47). They turn to 'Mr A and B to direct them how far to go in obeying Christ' (p. 48). And we can see the consequences in the fact that Christianity is no longer 'extending its domain' (p. 48). Human beings have a 'fatal tendency' to stop thinking about things once they are not considered 'doubtful' (p. 49).

This is not to say that beliefs always cease to be 'real and vital' once they are generally accepted (p. 49). And, as knowledge increases, there will, inevitably, be more and more issues that are no longer 'disputed' (p. 49). But having to defend a view against opponents does ensure a 'living apprehension' of its truth (p. 50). So, where there is unanimity of opinion, teachers need to impress upon their pupils 'the difficulties of the question' (p. 50). However, we seem to have lost the means of doing so. There is no modern-day equivalent of the '**Socratic dialectics**' or even of the medieval '**school disputations**', which required pupils to understand their own position through having to defend it (p. 50). No one's views should be regarded as knowledge, unless they have undergone 'the same mental process which would have been required of him in carrying on an active controversy with opponents' (p. 51).

In general, 'popular opinions' are neither completely true nor completely false, and we tend just to replace 'one partial and incomplete truth with another' (p. 52). 'Non-conforming' opinions are required to 'supply the remainder of the truth', and should be 'considered precious', even if they do sometimes contain 'error and confusion' (p. 52). For example, in the eighteenth century, most 'instructed' people were 'lost in admiration' of 'civilization', including science, literature and philosophy, and overrated the differences between modern and ancient times (p. 53). So, Rousseau's ideas exploded 'like bombshells', leading people to think again (p. 53). And although, on the whole, they were further from the truth than those he challenged, some of them, such as the emphasis on the 'superior worth' of a simple life, have survived (p. 53).

It is generally accepted that a 'healthy state of political life' requires both a 'party of order or stability' and one of 'progress or reform', with both deriving their 'utility from the deficiencies of the other' (p. 53). However, it is the other's opposition that keeps each 'within the limits of reason and sanity' (p. 53). Unless such opposed interests as, for example, **'democracy'** and **'aristocracy'**, 'property' and **'equality'**, 'liberty and **discipline**' are 'expressed with equal freedom', there is little prospect of both sides 'obtaining their due' (pp. 53–4). In the 'great practical concerns of life', truth is obtained through a 'reconciling and combining of opposites' (p. 54). This is accomplished through a struggle between 'combatants fighting under hostile banners', so we need to encourage the expression of minority opinions (p. 54). These are the opinions which are likely to be 'neglected'; but it is when people dissent from the world's 'apparent unanimity' that they probably have something worthwhile to say (p. 54).

It will be objected that some 'received principles', such as the precepts of '**Christian morality**', are 'more than half-truths' (p. 54). Let us consider this example. First, if we are talking about New Testament morality, it is hard to believe that it was intended as a 'complete' moral doctrine (p. 55). Its precepts, expressed in the 'most general' terms, concern specific ways of correcting or replacing the 'pre-existing morality' of the **Old Testament** (p. 55). Again, St Paul presupposes the pre-existing morality of 'the Greeks and Romans', urging Christians to conform to it (p. 55). In fact, Christian or 'theological' morality was worked out by the 'Catholic church', and was then adapted and modified by '**moderns** and **Protestants**' (p. 55). Our debt to Christian morality should not be underrated, but, in many respects, it is 'incomplete and one-sided' (p. 55).

A protest against paganism, it is 'negative rather than positive', teaching '**Abstinence from Evil**', rather than '**Pursuit of Good**' (p. 56). The main motives to 'a **virtuous life**' are 'the **hope of heaven and the threat of hell**', while it 'inculcates submission' to established authority (p. 56). The 'grand department of duty' is barely touched on; any ideas we have about our 'obligation to the public' derive from 'Greek and Roman sources' (p. 56). This is not to argue that the precepts Jesus taught cannot be reconciled with everything required by a 'comprehensive morality' (p. 57). But it is to say that his 'recorded deliverances' do not contain (because he did not intend them to) all 'the essential elements of the highest morality' (p. 57). Therefore, it is a mistake to look to them for a complete guide to life. Doing so, which often involves abandoning the 'secular standards' that have 'supplemented the Christian ethics', produces a 'servile type of character', submissive to what it considers to be God's will, but unable to grasp the 'conception of **Supreme Goodness**' (p. 57). Christianity's 'moral truths' need to be supplemented from other sources, underlining the point that 'the interests of truth require a diversity of opinions' (pp. 57–8).

I am not claiming that free discussion will cure the 'tendency of all opinions to become sectarian'; there will always be the 'impassioned **partisan**' of a particular point of view (p. 58). But it does have a 'salutary effect' on the 'disinterested bystander', because it enables him to hear both sides of the argument (p. 58). Truth's only chance is that 'every side of it' not only 'finds advocates, but is so advocated as to be listened to' (p. 59).

To recapitulate, there are four reasons why free expression of opinion is necessary for our 'mental well-being': a suppressed opinion may be true; if it is not completely true, it may contain some truth; even if the 'received opinion' is 'the whole truth', it will be held as 'a prejudice', with little understanding of its grounds, unless it is challenged; and it could become a mere dogma, losing its very meaning, and 'preventing the growth of any real and heartfelt conviction' (p. 59).

There are those who advocate free expression of opinions, as long as it does not 'pass the bounds of fair discussion' (p. 59). But where should we set such bounds? Every opponent of a point of view will be dubbed 'intemperate' by those whose opinion he questions, particularly if his arguments are 'telling and powerful' (p. 60). Sometimes, a person's manner of putting his case is 'objectionable', but this is the nature of controversy (p. 60). Usually, it is done in 'good faith', and it would be impossible to frame a law to deal with it (p. 60). Further, those who denounce 'invective, sarcasm, personality' and so on generally wish to prevent their use only against received opinions; they are happy for them to be employed against minority views (p. 60). All too often, their advocates are condemned as 'bad and immoral men': an accusation which unfairly damages their case, but which they are unable to use against their opponents, because it would 'recoil on their own cause' (pp. 61–2). And this method of defending prevailing opinions often deters the advocates of minority views from speaking out.

In general, if we had to choose, it would be more important, in the interests of 'truth and justice', to prevent 'offensive attacks' on the advocates of minority views than on the defenders of prevailing opinions (p. 61). Of course, 'law and authority have no business with restraining either' (p. 61) But, when engaging in controversy, we must practise 'the real morality of public discussion', striving for the highest standards of accuracy, candour and tolerance, and ensuring that we state what our opponents' opinions 'really are'; we must not exaggerate anything 'to their discredit', or conceal anything that is 'in their favour' (p. 61).

Chapter III (pp. 62–82)

Of Individuality, as One of the Elements of Well-Being

Do the reasons which make it 'imperative' for human beings to be free to form and express their opinions also require that they should be free to act on them: provided it is at 'their own risk and peril' (p. 62)? Nobody argues that 'actions should be as free as opinions' (p. 62). Indeed, even opinions cannot be expressed freely in situations where they might lead to a 'mischievous act' (p. 62). It is one thing to denounce corn-dealers as 'starvers of the poor' in the press, but another to do so to 'an excited mob', in front of a corn-dealer's house (p. 62). Acts that harm others usually need to be controlled, either by adverse public opinion or 'active interference' (p. 62). Individual liberty must be limited to the extent of preventing 'nuisance' to others, but only to that extent (p. 62). Human beings are not infallible, and, just as it is beneficial to have 'the fullest and freest comparison of opposite opinions', we also benefit from 'experiments' in different ways of living, which can test their worth (p. 63).

Unfortunately, when it comes to setting the boundaries between individual liberty and 'social control', the majority does not think that 'free development of **individuality**' has 'intrinsic worth' (p. 63). They are satisfied with the existing 'ways of mankind', and cannot understand why they do not suit everyone (p. 63). This is true even of 'moral and social reformers', who see individuality as a possible hindrance to acceptance of their proposed reforms (pp. 63–4). Few understand Wilhelm **von Humboldt**'s view that every human being should strive towards the fullest development of his individual powers, for which 'freedom, and variety of situations' are the essential requisites (p. 64).

I am not saying that the general view is that we should all just 'copy one another', or exclude from our way of life all elements of individual preference or judgement (p. 64). And, on the other hand, it would be 'absurd' for us to lead our lives as if there was nothing to be learned from past human experience (p. 64). But, as mature human beings, we do need to interpret this experience, so that we can apply it most appropriately to our own lives. Conforming to custom, just because it is custom, will not cultivate the distinctively human faculties of 'perception, judgement, discriminative feeling, mental activity, and . . . moral preference' (p. 65). And if we do not use these faculties, we will not develop them.

If we let the world choose our 'plan of life' for us, the only faculty we require is 'ape-like' imitation (p. 65). Such an approach may keep us out of harm's way, but it will do little for our 'comparative worth' as human beings (p. 66). We need to recognize the importance, not only of what we do, but of the sort of people we are. The most important of the 'works of man' is 'man himself' (p. 66). Let us imagine that all the things human beings have to do, from building houses to fighting battles, could be done by 'automatons' (p. 66). It would be a loss to swap even present humanity for such automatons, because we are not machines, built to a plan and programmed to carry out certain tasks, but living beings, capable of growth and development.

That our 'understanding should be our own', and that we should use our judgement, rather than blindly following custom, would probably be conceded (p. 66). However, this does not apply to 'desires and impulses', which are seen as dangerous (p. 66). But strong impulses are only dangerous when combined with weak **consciences**. Those with strong 'cultivated feelings' are capable of developing the 'most passionate love of virtue, and the sternest self-control' (p. 67). A person who has strong, controlled impulses possesses an 'energetic character'; and society needs such people (p. 67). Of course, past societies may have lacked the means of controlling such strong characters. But now the pendulum has swung too much the other way, and society has 'got the better of individuality' (p. 68). Even in what affects only themselves, people do not think about what they prefer, but of what is suitable to their position. Their only inclination is for 'what is customary'. But is this a 'desirable condition of human nature?' (p. 68).

Chapter III (pp. 62–82)

On the 'Calvinistic theory', which regards human nature as 'radically corrupt', and obeying 'the will of God' as the only purpose for which human faculties should be used, it is (pp. 68–9). This 'narrow theory of life' (which exists outside strict **Calvinism**) means that God would wish human beings to be 'cramped and dwarfed' in character (p. 69). But, if God is good, then surely he wants human beings to cultivate their faculties. There is an alternative to the Calvinist view, which treats human nature as having purposes other than **self-abnegation**: it is the 'Greek ideal of self-development', with which '**Platonic and Christian' ideals of self-government** can blend, but which they do not replace (pp. 69–70). It is by cultivating their individuality, within 'the limits imposed by the rights and interests of others', that human beings achieve their full potential (p. 70). And because, as we become more valuable to ourselves, we become more valuable to others, human life becomes 'rich, diversified, and animating' as a result (p. 70). It is no impediment to this process to be 'held to rigid rules of justice for the sake of others', because this teaches us concern for their welfare; but to be 'restrained' in things that do not affect their good 'dulls and blunts the whole nature' (p. 70).

But some will not be satisfied with the statement that 'cultivation of individuality' produces 'well-developed human beings' (p. 71). They will want to know what use such people are to 'undeveloped' people (p. 70). First, they can learn from them. Even the 'best beliefs and practices' eventually become purely 'mechanical', so society needs people 'of **originality**', to 'discover new truths' and to act as examples of 'enlightened conduct' (pp. 71–2). We have few **geniuses**, and they can only thrive 'in an *atmosphere* of freedom' (p. 72). Forced to squeeze themselves into one of society's 'moulds', they will be prevented from making their fullest possible contribution (p. 72). Society acknowledges genius as a 'fine thing' in theory, but in relation to 'thought and action', as opposed to, for example, painting or writing, generally considers it to be something it can 'do very well without' (p. 72). Indeed, 'unoriginal minds' cannot see the use of originality, and the more we need it, the less conscious we seem to be of the need (p. 73).

The general trend is 'to render mediocrity the ascendant power among mankind' (p. 73). These days, the world is ruled by public opinion, governments have become 'the organ of the tendencies and instincts of the masses', and the individual is 'lost in the crowd' (p. 73). Of course, public opinion means different things in different countries. In **America**, it means the 'whole white population'; in England, 'chiefly the middle class' (p. 73). But everywhere it means 'collective mediocrity', a mass whose thinking is done by the **newspapers**; and, in the 'present low state of the human mind', nothing better could be expected (pp. 73–4). Inevitably, the government of the mediocre is 'mediocre government'; no democratic government ever could rise above this level (p. 74). All 'wise or noble things' come from individuals, and it is to the credit of 'the average man' that he has been capable of responding to the leadership of great individuals (p. 74). I am not referring here to the 'strong man', who seizes control of government, because the 'power of compelling' both denies freedom to others and corrupts those who wield it (p. 74). But when, as at present, **mass opinion** has become 'the dominant power', the 'pronounced individuality' of those who occupy 'the higher eminences of thought' is crucially important (p. 74). And their being right is less important than their giving clear examples of not bending 'the knee to custom' (p. 74). As the 'tyranny of opinion' is so powerful, 'eccentricity' is desirable, in order to break it

(p. 74). Indeed, the current absence of eccentrics 'marks the chief danger of the time' (p. 75).

Independent action and disregard of custom are not to be encouraged just to find new ideas or values. It is also because there is simply no reason why human life should be 'constructed' on a single pattern (p. 75). Human beings can no more be satisfactorily kitted out with uniform ways of life than with coats of one size and style. Given the differences among human beings, they can be neither happy, nor develop their full intellectual and spiritual potential, unless there is 'corresponding diversity in their modes of life' (p. 75). It is not as if diversity is discouraged in activities which do not matter. It is equally acceptable to like or dislike rowing or smoking, for example. But the man, and particularly the woman, who does 'what nobody does', is immediately condemned (p. 76). The problem is that the majority is 'moderate' in both intellect and inclination, has no strong desire to do anything unusual, and so cannot understand those who have (p. 76). In addition, there is the present strong movement for 'the improvement of morals', which, though '**philanthropic**' in spirit, causes people to 'prescribe general rules of conduct' and to desire everyone to comply with the 'approved standard' (p. 77).

The consequence is that almost the only 'outlet for energy' left in England is business, and people are encouraged to spend their remaining time on hobbies (p. 78). We have become 'individually small', but it was 'men of another stamp' who made the country great, and who will be needed to 'prevent its decline' (p. 78). The 'despotism of custom' is the enemy of 'human advancement', because it stands in the way of anything better than the customary (p. 78). The 'whole **East**' shows what happens when custom's despotism 'is complete' (p. 78). Progress stops, unless there is liberty and individuality.

In **Europe**, becoming subject to the rule of custom would not have quite the same effect. Although '**singularity**' is deplored, change is not ruled out, provided it applies to everyone (p. 79). Indeed, we are eager for change and improvement in 'politics, in **education**, even in morals', and consider ourselves to be 'the most progressive people who ever lived' (p. 79). It is not progress to which we are opposed, but individuality. We try to make 'ourselves all alike', failing to realize that it is human differences which enable us to perceive our own strengths and weaknesses (p. 79). The history of **China** illustrates the dangers of discouraging individuality. If all our thoughts and actions are governed by 'the same **maxims** and rules', we become 'stationary' (p. 80).

What is it that tends to prevent this happening in Europe? It is our 'remarkable diversity of character and culture' (p. 80). 'Individuals, classes, nations' have gone their own way, and, although they may have been 'intolerant' of each other, they have not been able to prevent each other's individual development (p. 80). As a result, Europe has achieved 'progressive and many-sided development' (p. 80). But this diversity is diminishing. **De Tocqueville** notes how, in the present generation, one Frenchman closely resembles another; and this is even more true of the English. Freedom and 'variety of situations' are necessary for human development, but it is ever harder to find the second (p. 81). In the past, individuals from different classes, professions or parts of the country lived almost in 'different worlds' (p. 81). Now, so many people read the same things, visit the same places, and have the same 'hopes and fears' (p. 80). And there are many factors in modern society to encourage this trend. Political changes, improvements in communications and increased commercial activity do so, as does the extension of education, which brings people under 'common influences' and gives all access to the same 'general stock of facts and **sentiments**' (p. 80). But the most powerful factor of all is 'the ascendancy of public opinion in the State' (pp. 81–2). As politicians give up any idea of resisting 'the will of the public', support for any kind of 'nonconformity' is disappearing (p. 82).

The influences 'hostile to Individuality' are extremely powerful (p. 82). The trend towards 'enforced assimilation' can only be resisted if 'intelligent' people recognize the value of individuality, and are prepared to stand up for it, even when particular individual differences seem pointless or even 'for the worse' (p. 82). If we wait too long, all deviations from the 'one uniform type' will come to be seen as 'impious, immoral, even monstrous and contrary to nature' (p. 82).

Chapter IV (pp. 83–103)

Of the Limits to the Authority of Society Over the Individual

Where should the boundary be drawn between individual 'sovereignty' and 'the authority of society' (p. 83)? What mainly concerns individuals should 'belong' to them, while society should control that part 'which chiefly interests' it (p. 83). Society is not based on a '**contract**', but all those who receive society's protection owe its other members a 'return for the benefit' (p. 83). They must not harm other people's interests, and they must play their part in defending them 'from injury' (p. 83). Again, if individuals act in a way which, though not illegal, damages other people's welfare, they may be 'punished by opinion' (p. 83). However, when a person's conduct affects only his own interests, there is no justification for interference. That person must be allowed 'to do the action and stand the consequences' (p. 84).

This is not an argument for 'selfish indifference' towards other people (p. 84). But 'whips and scourges' are not the only means of persuading people 'to their good' (p. 84). Of course, we should encourage each other to develop 'self-regarding virtues', so that we select the 'wise instead of foolish' course of action (p. 84). However, we are not entitled to say to another human being that he shall not do 'what he chooses' with his own life (p. 84). In this area, 'Individuality has its proper field of action', and all the mistakes a person is likely to make by ignoring advice are 'far outweighed by the evil' of others being able to force him into a course of action for what they judge to be his good (p. 85).

It is the case, though, that if a person shows 'folly' in the way he leads his life, he will become 'a subject of distaste' (p. 85). We should point out his faults to such a person, and we are entitled to warn others against him. One who cannot live within his means, or who recklessly 'pursues animal pleasures', must expect others to have a low opinion of him (p. 86). But the 'unfavourable judgement' of others should be the sole penalty a person faces for actions that affect only 'his own good', and do not harm 'the interests of others' (pp. 86–7). However, actions which are 'injurious to others', such as encroaching on their rights, or treating them unfairly, and the 'dispositions' that underlie them, such as 'malice' and 'envy', should attract 'moral retribution and punishment' (p. 87). But we must always bear in mind that society is not entitled to enforce a so-called 'duty to oneself', which is just another name for 'self-respect' (p. 87). If a person 'spoils his life by mismanagement', we must not treat him 'like an enemy of society'; the most we are entitled to do is to avoid his company

(p. 88). But if a person breaks the rules 'necessary for the protection of others', society, as the 'protector of all its members', should punish him (p. 88).

Now some people do not accept the distinction between that 'part of a person's life which concerns only himself, and that which concerns others' (p. 88). They contend that no part of a person's conduct is 'a matter of indifference' to other members of society: even if it is just a matter of a bad example being set (p. 88). Further, even if they harm only themselves, does not society have a duty to protect people from the consequences of their actions, when they show themselves incapable of managing their own affairs? This would not stop 'new and original experiments in living', only prevent actions that have been 'tried and condemned' throughout history (p. 89).

Of course, if an individual's actions do break obligations to others, they can no longer be treated as **'self-regarding'** (p. 90). For example, a person, who, through **'intemperance'**, was unable to pay his debts or look after his family, would rightly be subject to 'moral disapprobation' (p. 90). But where conduct breaks no 'specific duty', and harms only the individual himself, society must endure it 'for the sake of the greater good of human freedom' (p. 91). After all, society controls the education of the young; it has only itself to blame if it fails to bring them up as responsible citizens. Furthermore, attempts to force people into 'prudence or temperance' will often cause them to rebel (p. 92).

Perhaps, the strongest argument against interference with 'purely personal conduct' is that it usually just means the majority view of 'what is good' being imposed on the minority (pp. 92–3). It is easy to imagine an ideal world, in which people only required others to refrain from behaviour condemned by 'universal experience' (p. 93). But where would 'a public', capable of such restraint, be found (p. 93)? And it is easy to illustrate the dangers of allowing the 'moral police' to encroach upon the 'legitimate liberty of the individual' (p. 94). What if those who have moral or religious objections to such 'amusements' as dancing, public games and the theatre obtained a parliamentary majority, and attempted to ban, or curtail, such activities (p. 96)? There would be an outcry; and so there should be if ever a government tries to stop people enjoying 'any pleasure which they think wrong' (p. 96). Again, a **democratic constitution**', and a 'considerable diffusion of Socialist opinions', might result in the 'notion that the public has a right to a veto on the manner in which individuals shall spend their incomes' and attempts to restrict property ownership (p. 97).

But we are not confined to 'suppositious cases'; there are actual examples of 'gross usurpations upon the liberty of private life' (p. 98). In parts of the United States, the campaign against intemperance has resulted in people not being allowed to buy '**fermented drinks**' (p. 98). In this country, a representative of the '**Alliance**', in a letter to Lord **Stanley**, claimed that, while matters of 'thought, opinion, conscience' were outside the sphere of legislation, those relating to 'social act, habit, relation' were within it (pp. 98–9). However, there is a third category, 'acts and habits which are not social, but individual'; and it is to this category that drinking alcohol belongs (p. 99). However, the supporters of the **temperance movement** argue that trade in alcohol 'invades' their '**social rights**', because it may create social disorder and demoralize society (p. 99). But these so-called 'social rights' seem to amount to a demand that the government legislate to remove the 'grievance' of other people not doing as the temperance movement wishes (p. 99). There is no 'violation of liberty' that so 'monstrous a principle' could not be used to justify (p. 99). Even the expression of an opinion they consider 'noxious' might be deemed to invade their 'social rights' (pp. 99–100). Another example of 'illegitimate interference' with individual liberty is '**Sabbatarian** legislation' (p. 100). While it may be 'allowable and right' for the law to 'guarantee' a day of leisure for the benefit of all citizens, this does not apply to how the day of leisure is spent; so there should be no restrictions on Sunday 'amusements' (p. 100). And if some choose to work on Sunday, to provide entertainment for others, they should be allowed to do so. The only grounds for banning such entertainment are religious; and the idea that it is one person's duty to ensure that another is religious is 'the foundation of all the **religious persecutions** ever perpetrated' (p. 101). Then again, we have 'the language of downright persecution' directed by the press in this country against **Mormonism** (p. 101). No one has a 'deeper disapprobation than I' of a religious teaching that infringes the 'principle of liberty' through the practice of **polygamy** (p. 102). But the women who submit to this do so voluntarily. And, unless our assistance is called for by those who are suffering under this arrangement, we are not entitled to interfere, except by speaking out against it. But, perhaps, we are afraid that 'barbarism' will 'revive and conquer civilization' (p. 103). For this to be a danger, our civilization must, indeed, have become '**degenerate**' (p. 103).

Chapter V (pp. 105–28)

Applications

There are 'two maxims which together form the entire doctrine of this Essay': an individual is not accountable for actions which concern only his own interests, but he is, and may be subjected to 'social or to legal punishment' for, actions harmful to the interests of others (p. 104). This is not to say that society's interference is always justified in the latter case; they may be caused by 'bad social institutions', as when some people succeed in 'an overcrowded profession', and 'benefit' from the failure of others (pp. 104–5). It would not be in society's interests to interfere on behalf of the 'disappointed competitors', unless 'fraud' had been practised (p. 105). Again, 'trade is a social act', and it used to be the general view that governments should regulate it closely (p. 105). However, after 'a long struggle', it is now accepted that the most effective way to ensure the 'cheapness and good quality of goods' is to have '**Free Trade**' (p. 105). However, the 'the principle of individual liberty asserted in this Essay' is not involved in the so-called 'doctrine of Free Trade', any more than it is in questions of whether society should require 'sanitary precautions' or safety arrangements for those in dangerous jobs (pp. 105–6). While it is better to let people make their own decisions about such matters, it is legitimate for governments to regulate them. However, trade does raise issues that bear on individual liberty, as with laws banning the sale of alcohol (p. 106).

The issue of the sale of poisons raises the question of the 'proper limits' of police powers (p. 106). To what extent may individual liberty be 'invaded' to prevent crime or accident (p. 106)? Governments have a duty to prevent crime, but it is easily abused 'to the prejudice of liberty' (p. 106). Poisons are not used only to commit murder. They may be bought for 'innocent' purposes, and restrictions on their sale will affect such purchasers (p. 106). So what sort of regulations are compatible with individual liberty? Labels stating their 'dangerous character' would be acceptable, but requiring a medical practitioner's certificate would make it much harder to buy poisons for 'legitimate uses' (p. 107). One approach would be to require the sellers of poisons to keep a record of purchasers and why they needed the poison.

Society's right to prevent crime by 'antecedent precautions' shows the limitations of the maxim that 'purely self-regarding conduct' cannot be interfered with to prevent or punish crime (p. 108). For example, governments should not legislate against drunkenness. However, if someone was convicted of violent acts against others while drunk, society can legitimately ban that person from drinking, and punish him if he becomes drunk again. Similarly, people cannot be punished for idleness, but if, as a result, they fail to support their children, society is entitled to compel them to do so. There are acts, such as 'offences against decency', which, if done in private, harm only the agents (pp. 108–9). However, if done publicly, they offend others, and society rightly prohibits this.

Respect for individual liberty may require that a 'blameable' action be permitted, because its consequences harm only the agent (p. 109). However, should a person be allowed to incite others to commit such an act? This is a difficult question. To incite someone to commit an act is not 'strictly a case of self-regarding conduct'; it is a 'social act' (p. 109). However, the reasons on which the 'principle of individual liberty' is based do apply to it (p. 109). If people are to be free to do as they judge best in matters affecting only themselves, they must also be free to consult others. The only exception may be if the instigator derives 'a personal benefit from his advice' (p. 109). This raises the whole question of how we deal with people whose whole 'mode of living' involves promoting acts that are considered contrary to the public good (p. 109). Respect for individual liberty requires us to tolerate **fornication** and gambling, but should we tolerate a '**pimp**', or the running of a '**gambling-house**' (pp. 109–10)? On 'the side of toleration', it could be argued that, if an act is self-regarding, and is itself permitted, society has no right to stop people persuading others to do it, or providing them with the means of doing so (p. 110). On the other hand, it is argued that, even though an act is permitted, if society regards the act as 'bad', it is entitled to remove 'the influence' of those who, for self-interested reasons, encourage others to perform it (p. 110)? So, although laws against gambling may be 'utterly indefensible', and there should be no restrictions on people gambling in their own homes, 'gambling-houses should not be permitted' (p. 110). Such cases are very difficult to decide. It is clear, though, that banning the sale of alcohol, as by the '**Maine Law**', just because it can be used 'in excess', is an infringement of personal liberty: it prevents its sale for 'legitimate use' (p. 111). However, the interest that sellers of alcohol have in promoting 'intemperance' justifies government regulation of its sale (p. 111).

Should government discourage conduct which is 'contrary to the best interests of the agent', as by imposing heavy taxes on alcohol (p. 111)? Taxing alcohol, just to make it harder to obtain, differs 'only in degree' from banning it, and will mean that some people will be unable to afford it (p. 111). However, the state needs to raise revenue through taxation, and some taxation has to be 'indirect' (p. 112). Taxes must be levied on some 'commodities', and government has a duty to tax those which 'the consumers can best spare'; so, on this basis, taxing alcohol is 'not only admissible, but to be approved of' (p. 112). What about the question of restricting the right to sell these commodities? It depends on the motive. To do so in order to prevent '**breaches of the peace**' is acceptable, but not if the intention is to reduce sales (p. 112). This is to treat people like 'children' (p. 113).

The liberty of the individual, in matters which concern only himself, implies the liberty of groups of individuals to 'regulate by mutual agreement such things as regard them jointly' (p. 113). There is no difficulty with this, although it may be necessary for them to make mutually binding engagements. However, in this, as in other 'civilized countries', it is not possible for people to be held to engagements which 'violate the rights of third parties', or which are 'injurious to themselves' (p. 113). For example, if a person undertook to sell himself into slavery, the agreement would be 'null and void' (p. 113). This is because 'the principle of freedom cannot require that he should be free not to be free' (p. 114). And there should be provision for those who have bound themselves to each other to be released from their agreement. Indeed, Baron von Humboldt maintains that engagements involving 'personal relations or services' should be of limited duration (p. 114). He has also argued that a marriage should require only the declared wish of either partner to dissolve it, because 'its objects are frustrated unless the feelings of both parties are in harmony' (p. 114). However, the issue is not that simple. When a person marries, he creates expectations about his future conduct, and thus incurs 'moral obligations' towards his partner (p. 115). There may also be children involved. Although it may be the case that these considerations should not affect people's *'legal* freedom' to end their marriage, they do limit their *'moral* freedom' to do so (p. 115).

Of course, while liberty is often 'withheld where it should be granted', it is sometimes granted where it should not be (p. 116). A person should not be 'free to do as he likes in acting for another' (p. 116). However, society permits husbands to exercise 'almost despotic power' over their wives; wives need to have the same legal rights as 'all other persons' (p. 116). Again, there is strong opposition to even 'the smallest interference of law' with a father's control of his children (p. 116). We say that parents have a duty to ensure that their children receive an education, but the state is reluctant to do as it ought, and pass a law compelling them to do so.

Yet, if the government decided to '*require* for every child a good education, it might save itself the trouble of *providing* one' (p. 117). The state's role would be confined to meeting the educational costs of children whose parents could not afford to pay fees, and what the state should or should not teach would cease to be a 'battlefield for **sects** and parties' (p. 117). Certainly, I am against entrusting the education of its people to the state, because a 'general **State education** is a mere contrivance for moulding people to be exactly like one another', with the mould reflecting the 'predominant power in the government' (pp. 117–18). Individuality and diversity of opinion require 'diversity of education' (p. 117). At most, state education should only exist as 'one among many competing experiments' (p. 118).

And the law requiring parents to educate their children should be enforced through annual '**public examinations**' for all children from an early age; and if a child is unable to read at the appropriate age, the parent should be fined (p. 118). The range of examination subjects would be gradually extended, to ensure the acquisition of 'a certain minimum of general knowledge', with opportunities to take higher level 'voluntary examinations' (p. 118). However, to stop the state influencing opinions, these examinations would be 'confined to facts and positive science' (p. 119). So, those in religion and politics would not be about the truth of a religious belief or political principle, but about their content and which parties or religious groups hold them. All attempts by the state to influence its citizens' views on 'disputed topics' are 'evil', but it is entitled to try to equip them with sufficient knowledge to reach their own conclusions (p. 119). However, there should be no question of governments excluding people from following a particular profession, including teaching, just because they have not passed examinations at a sufficiently high level.

In an overpopulated country, such as ours, having children without being able to support them is a 'serious offence' against society (p. 120). Laws, such as those in some European countries, which forbid a couple to marry, unless they can prove possession of the means of providing for a family, 'do not exceed the legitimate powers of the State' (p. 120). They prevent 'an act injurious to others' (p. 120). How extraordinary it is that 'current ideas of liberty', which permit 'real infringements' of liberty, baulk at attempts to stop actions that will impose lives of 'wretchedness' on the unfortunate children (p. 120).

Finally, moving away from issues of interference with individual liberty, is it acceptable for government to help its citizens, rather than leaving them to fend for themselves? There are three objections. First, no one is better fitted to 'conduct any business' than those who have a personal interest in it (p. 121). Second, even if government could carry out the function better, it is desirable to allow the people concerned to do it themselves for their 'mental education' (p. 121). This is a good reason for having '**jury trial**', '**municipal institutions**' and '**voluntary associations**' (p. 121). These institutions and activities provide 'training' in citizenship, by accustoming people to act from 'public or semi-public motives', and thus help to create social cohesion (pp. 121–2). Indeed, it is debatable whether a 'free constitution' can be sustained without local government and private ownership and management of industry (p. 122). Government 'operations' tend to be the same everywhere, but with 'individuals and voluntary associations', there are experiments and 'diversity of experience' (p. 122). What the state can do, however, is to circulate information about these various experiments.

Third, 'interference' by government should be restricted because of the 'great evil' of adding to its power (p. 122). The more government functions increase, the more likely it is that many 'active and ambitious' citizens will become its 'hangers-on' (p. 122). If our great institutions, such as the railways, banks, insurance companies, industrial concerns, universities, charities, 'municipal corporations and local boards', all became 'departments of the **central** administration', with their employees paid by the government, and looking to it for advancement, 'not all the freedom of the press and **popular constitution** of the **legislature** would make this or any other country free otherwise than in name' (pp. 122–3). Recently, a '**competitive examination**' has been proposed for entry into the **civil service**, to ensure recruitment of the most able people (p. 123). Opponents of this proposal have argued that the civil service offers insufficient reward for the 'highest talents', who will find better prospects elsewhere (p. 123). But this is the new system's 'safety valve' (p. 123). If the country's best talent could be 'concentrated in a numerous **bureaucracy**', to which everybody else looked 'for all things', no reform could ever be introduced which harmed its interests (pp. 123–4).

This is the situation in Russia, where the '**Czar** himself is powerless against the bureaucratic body' (p. 124). He can send any one of them to **Siberia**, but he cannot govern without them. They can veto every decree by simply not carrying it out. In the United States, on the other hand, people are used to conducting 'every kind of civil business' (p. 124). If they found themselves without a government, any group of Americans would be able to 'improvise' one (p. 124). This is how a 'free people' should be, and no bureaucracy could make such people do 'anything that they do not like' (pp. 124–5). But where everything is 'done through the bureaucracy', nothing it opposes can be carried out (p. 125). The 'constitution of such countries' (and China is a good example) exists to recruit and organize its most able citizens into a 'disciplined body' to govern the rest (p. 125). And the more successful such a system is, the more complete is the 'bondage' of all citizens (including members of the bureaucracy) to it (p. 125). It is easy, too, for such extensive bureaucracies to sink into 'indolent routine' (p. 125). The more bureaucratic a government becomes, the greater the need for there to be a well-organized and well-informed group of able people outside the government, who will keep its activities under review, and point out its mistakes.

Indeed, in order to reap the full benefits of 'centralized power', without handing over 'too great a proportion' of administrative activity to central government, we should abide by the principle of: 'the greatest **dissemination** of power consistent with efficiency, but the greatest possible centralization of information, and diffusion from the centre' (p. 126). To assist 'municipal administration', there should be a 'central superintendence' department, which would gather information from local authorities in this country and abroad, and disseminate it to local government officers; and which would also ensure that they obeyed 'the law laid down for their guidance' (pp. 126–7). This would be analogous to the relationship between the **Poor Law Board** and local 'administrators of the

Poor Rate' (p. 127). Governments cannot have too much information, which 'aids and stimulates, individual exertion and development' (p. 127). Where things go wrong is government substituting its own activity for that of its citizens. The 'worth of a State' is that of the 'individuals composing it' (p. 128). If a state, however good its intentions, 'dwarfs' its people, in order to turn them into its 'docile instruments', it will find that it has created citizens who can accomplish little (p. 128). It may perfect the machinery of government, but, for this machinery to work effectively, the 'vital power' of its citizens is required (p. 128).

Overview

The following section is a chapter-by-chapter overview of the five chapters in John Stuart Mill's *On Liberty*, designed for quick reference to the detailed summary above. Readers may also find this overview section helpful for revision.

Chapter 1 Introductory (pp. 5–19)

Mill explains that *On Liberty* concerns the important issue of how much power society should be able to exercise over the individual. In the past, this question had been discussed in the context of people trying to obtain freedom from undemocratic governments, whose interests were clearly opposed to theirs. However, with the arrival of more democratic systems of government, conflict of interest between government and governed no longer seemed inevitable. The view had gained ground that, as elected governments represent the people, there need be no restrictions on their powers.

But it is not so straightforward. Democracy can give rise to the tyranny of the majority, which means that individual liberty still requires protection. There is also social tyranny, by which society tries to impose its ideas on dissenting minorities and individuals. It is vitally important to determine the extent to which it is legitimate for either governments or public opinion to interfere with individual independence.

Mill asks where the boundary should be drawn, and regrets the lack of interest in the question. Even social reformers are more concerned with promoting their own ideas than with defending individual freedom. The exception is religion. In many countries, the inability of any one religious group to achieve dominance has meant religious groups agreeing to differ. But even here, most strongly religious people have reservations about toleration, and full religious freedom is only found where there is indifference to religion.

Mill maintains that England differs from most continental countries, in that the law is less prescriptive of individual behaviour. But, with the growth of democracy, this could change, so an accepted principle for determining the legitimacy of any interference with individual conduct is needed. And he wishes to put forward a simple principle to regulate it: that the only purpose for which power can rightfully be exercised over any member of a civilized community, against his will, is to prevent harm to others. This principle of liberty means that the individual is only accountable to society for conduct affecting others; his own good is not sufficient justification for interference. Individual human liberty embraces the whole area of opinion, thought, feeling and conscience, including free expression of opinion. It is an essential characteristic of a free society that people are able to pursue their chosen way of life, despite others' disapproval, provided it does not harm them. But this view runs counter to the trend of both legislation and public opinion, which is to strengthen social control at the expense of individual freedom.

Chapter II   *Of the Liberty of Thought and Discussion* *(pp. 20–61)*

Mill hopes that no arguments are necessary in defence of press freedom. Indeed, in countries with some measure of democracy, attempts by government to control the press are unlikely: unless public opinion demands it. But this would not justify such control. Preventing an opinion being expressed robs the whole human race. If it is right, error goes uncorrected; if it is wrong, the opportunity is lost of seeing truth confirmed through collision with error.

But people are willing to allow opinions to be suppressed, because they place too much reliance on their own; and it makes no difference to them that previous generations held, or other people hold, different ones. Again, it is argued that stopping erroneous opinions being propagated is not to claim infallibility. Governments and individuals would be wrong to permit the circulation of opinions harmful to society's welfare. However, Mill rejects this argument. Most human opinions are rational mainly because they can be corrected through discussion. The problem today is that people are not so much convinced of their opinions as convinced of being lost without them. Governments are urged not to allow socially useful opinions to be challenged, but no opinion is useful, unless true. Mill considers the example of opinions about God's existence. To be sure that God exists is not to claim infallibility, but attempting to decide the matter for others, without letting them hear the contrary arguments, is. It should be remembered that Socrates was put to death for denying the existence of the gods recognized by the state, while Jesus himself was executed for blasphemy. The Emperor Marcus Aurelius, one of history's most enlightened rulers, persecuted Christians to protect existing religious beliefs which, in his view, were keeping society together.

Mill concedes that those who put forward new opinions are no longer killed, but, in England, the social stigma attaching to unorthodox views on matters such as religion inhibits expression of them. And it is not only that people's mental development is limited by not allowing different points of view to be discussed freely. A received opinion may be true but, unless questioned, it becomes a mere dogma. To know and understand our side of the argument, we need to hear opposing ones. Further, history shows that once religious or ethical ideas are generally accepted, interest in them declines, as is the case with Christianity. As a result, Christianity is no longer a dynamic, growing religion.

Increasing knowledge will mean fewer disputed questions but, on most subjects, popular opinions are neither right nor wrong; dissentient views are needed to provide the rest of the truth. Minority opinions are particularly important, because they often represent neglected points of view. The example of Christian moral teaching underlines the importance of diversity of points of view. Some claim that Christianity provides a complete guide to life but, in fact, it needs to be supplemented by Greek and Roman morality, which place a greater emphasis on the ideas of duty and public obligation.

Mill's conclusion is that there are four reasons why free expression of opinion is necessary: a suppressed opinion may be true; if it is not completely true, it may contain some truth; even if the accepted opinion is the whole truth, unless challenged, it will be held without conviction; and, in the end, understanding of the reasons on which it is based will be lost. He rejects the view that opinions should only be expressed freely if this is done with restraint, and deplores the fact that the advocates of unorthodox views are often condemned as immoral, thus unfairly discrediting their arguments. It is more important that society protects the opponents of prevailing opinions than their defenders.

Chapter III *Of Individuality, as One of the Elements of Well-Being (pp. 62–82)*

Mill asks if people should be free to act on their opinions, as well as form and express them. Actions cannot be as free as opinions, and acts harmful to others should incur adverse public opinion or be prevented. However, when the boundaries between individual liberty and social control are fixed, it is clear that most people are not interested in having opportunities for the free development of individuality. But conforming to custom, for its own sake, will not develop such human faculties as perception, mental activity and moral judgement.

People should not let society decide how they should lead their lives. They should use their own judgement, not simply follow custom. They need to embrace the Greek ideal of self-development and, while respecting others' rights and interests, cultivate their individuality, in order to become well-developed human beings. Society needs people, capable of original thinking, who can discover new truths, and act as examples to others; but such people can only thrive in an atmosphere of freedom.

However, Mill thinks that contemporary society is not conducive to the cultivation of individuality and originality. This is because people allow the newspapers to do their thinking for them, so public opinion favours mediocrity and customary ideas; and democratic governments are afraid to challenge public opinion. Inevitably, the government of the mediocre is mediocre government. The best ideas come from individuals so, in an era dominated by mass opinion, the cultivation of individuality, and the example of those who refuse to defer to custom, even if they are wrong, is crucially important.

Independent action is not only important for discovering

new ideas. There is no reason why human life should be based on a single pattern. Human beings differ, and can only develop their full potential, and be happy, if they can choose their own way of life. However, the current emphasis on so-called moral improvement means that those who do as nobody else does are condemned for not conforming to the approved standard of conduct. But the despotism of custom obstructs human progress, which can only flourish in conditions of freedom and individuality.

Mill does not deny that, in Europe, change in such areas as politics, education and morals, is welcomed; but only if it applies to everyone. It is individuality, not change, which is deplored. But, in trying to make themselves alike, human beings fail to recognize that, if they are all governed by the same ideas and principles, progress ceases. Europe's great cultural and social diversity has stimulated progress, but this diversity is diminishing, because so many people read the same books and newspapers, receive much the same sort of education, and are exposed to the influence of the same, ascendant public opinion. It will only be possible to resist the trend towards uniformity, if intelligent people recognize the value of individuality.

Chapter IV   *Of the Limits to the Authority of Society Over the Individual (pp. 83–103)*

Mill asks where the boundary between individual freedom and legitimate social control of individual conduct should be drawn. Individuals should control what concerns them, while society should control that part of conduct which chiefly concerns it. Members of society must not harm the interests of others, and must play their part in defending them from harm. And, if individuals behave in ways that, though not illegal, damage other people's welfare, they may be punished by adverse public opinion. But when a person's conduct affects only his own interests, no interference is justified; the person must be free to act, and take the consequences.

People should be encouraged to develop self-regarding virtues, so that they make wise, not foolish, choices, and it is legitimate to point out their mistakes to those who mismanage their lives by, for example, failing to live within their means, or indulging in animal pleasures. But the evil of forcing people to act against their wishes is greater than any mistakes they may make as a result of choosing for themselves. On the other hand, such actions as encroaching on people's rights, or treating them unfairly, which cause them harm, deserve moral retribution and punishment.

Mill notes that some people reject the distinction between that part of a person's life which concerns only himself and that which concerns others, on the grounds that society is affected by every part of a person's conduct. Even if people harm only themselves, society should protect them from the consequences. Mill accepts that actions that break obligations to others, as when a heavy drinker is unable to provide for his family, cannot be treated as purely self-regarding. But for the sake of human freedom, society must endure conduct by which the individual harms only himself.

One of the most powerful arguments against interference with purely personal conduct is that it usually means imposing the majority view of what is good on the minority. The dangers of allowing the legitimate liberty of the individual to be invaded can be illustrated by imagining what would happen if opponents of dancing, public games or the theatre obtained a parliamentary majority, and tried to ban them.

There would be an outcry, as there should be if any government attempted to stop people enjoying pleasures of which it disapproved. But there are actual examples of such behaviour, as with the ban on the sale of alcohol in parts of the United States. Representatives of the temperance movement argue that their social rights are invaded by the sale of alcohol, as it may lead to social disorder. But any violation of individual liberty could be justified on this basis.

Mill draws attention to the intemperate language with which Mormonism is denounced in the British press. He agrees that its polygamy is deplorable, but it is engaged in voluntarily. The language used suggests a fear that barbarism will revive, and destroy civilization. But a civilization would need to be in a very decayed condition for this to happen.

Chapter V Applications (pp. 105–28)

For Mill, the whole argument of *On Liberty* can be summed up in two maxims: an individual is not accountable to society for any actions affecting only his own interests, but he is accountable (and may be punished) for those which harm the interests of others. There are also areas where issues of individual liberty do not arise, as, for example, in such questions as free trade, or legal enforcement of safety arrangements for those in dangerous occupations. Generally, it is better to let people make their own decisions about such matters, but it is legitimate for governments to regulate them.

The sale of poisons raises the question of the proper limits of police powers. Should individual liberty be invaded to prevent crime or accident? Poisons can be used to commit murder, but restrictions on their sale must be compatible with individual liberty, and not prevent people buying them for legitimate purposes. Indeed society's right to prevent crime, by taking precautions against it, shows the limitations of the maxim that purely self-regarding conduct cannot be interfered with. A government has no right to ban drunkenness, but if someone is convicted of behaving violently towards others while drunk, society can legitimately ban him from drinking.

Respect for individual liberty means society permitting actions of which it disapproves, because the consequences affect only the agent, but Mill considers the difficult question of whether people should be allowed to encourage others to commit such acts. Encouraging someone to do something is a social act, but, if people are to be free to act as they wish in matters affecting only themselves, they must also be free to consult others. However, what happens if the instigator derives a benefit from the encouragement he gives? There are those, such as pimps and casino owners, whose whole way of life depends upon promoting acts considered contrary to the public good. Mill acknowledges the difficulty of the question. On the one hand, society appears to have no right to stop people persuading others to commit a self-regarding act, such as fornication or gambling, which is itself permitted; on the other, is not society entitled to remove the influence of those who, for self-interested reasons, encourage others to perform acts it condemns? He thinks that banning the sale of alcohol, due to possible excessive use, clearly infringes personal liberty, because it prevents its sale for legitimate purposes. However, the sellers' commercial interest in encouraging overindulgence justifies government regulation of its sale.

But should governments discourage consumption of alcohol by levying high taxes on it? There is only a difference of degree between banning alcohol and taxing it heavily, in order to make it harder to obtain. However, the state needs tax revenue, and some taxation has to be indirect. Government should tax non-essential items so, on this basis, it is right to tax alcohol. Again, it is legitimate to restrict the right to sell alcohol to prevent breaches of the peace, but not just to reduce sales, which would involve treating people like children.

Individual freedom implies the freedom of groups of individuals to make mutually binding agreements: but not ones that invade the rights of third parties, or which are damaging to themselves. For example, any agreement a person made to sell himself into slavery would be null and void. The principle of freedom cannot require that a person should be free not to be free. Mill considers the argument that it should require only the declared wish of either partner to dissolve a marriage, but feels that, by marrying, a person incurs moral obligations towards his partner, while children may be involved. It may be the case that these considerations should not affect people's legal freedom to end a marriage, but they do limit their moral freedom to do so.

Mill argues that liberty is often denied where it should be allowed, and allowed where it should not be. Nobody should be free to do as he likes when acting for another, but society grants husbands almost despotic power over their wives. Wives should have full legal rights. There is always strong opposition to the slightest interference with paternal control of children. Parents have a duty to ensure that their children are educated, but the state is unwilling to pass a law compelling them to do so. Yet, if the government required that every child receive good education, it would not need to provide education itself, limiting the state's role to meeting the educational costs of children whose parents could not afford school fees. He is opposed to state-provided education, which just moulds people to be exactly like each other; individuality and diversity of opinion require diversity of educational provision.

A law compelling parents to educate their children should be enforced through annual public examinations, with penalties for parents whose children do not reach the required standard. A widening range of subjects would ensure acquisition of a basic level of general knowledge. There would also be voluntary higher-level examinations, but these would test only facts, not opinions. The state should not try to influence its citizens' opinions, but it has the right to equip them with sufficient knowledge to reach their own conclusions. However, governments should not exclude people from following a particular profession, including teaching, just because they have not passed a particular examination. Mill also argues that, in overpopulated countries like England, having children, without being able to support them, is an offence against society. Therefore, it would be legitimate for the state to pass laws forbidding a couple to marry, unless they can prove they have the means to provide for a family.

Mill asks if it is acceptable for a government to help its citizens, rather than leaving them to fend for themselves. There are three objections: First, no one is better equipped to do something than those with a personal interest in it. Second, even if government could perform the task better, people are more likely to develop into responsible citizens if they do things for themselves. It would be difficult to sustain a free society without, for example, local government, jury trial and voluntary associations, which help to train people in citizenship. Third, government interference should be limited, because of the evil of adding to its power. If such institutions as banks, insurance companies, industrial concerns, universities, charities and local councils were all run by central government, and operated by state employees, neither a free press nor a democratic constitution could make the country really free. If (as in China), the country's most able people were to be employed in a state bureaucracy, on which everybody else depended, nothing that it opposed could be done, and no reform, contrary to its interests, could be implemented. The more successful such a system was, the more completely it would enslave all the country's citizens.

Mill believes that, to derive most benefit from an effective central government, without giving it too much power, there should be as much devolution of power from the centre as is consistent with efficiency, while central government should be responsible for gathering information from a wide range or sources, and disseminating it to local authorities. Information, to aid and stimulate individual and local effort, is valuable, but things go wrong if government substitutes its own activity for that of its citizens. A state is as good as its citizens. If (albeit with good intentions) it tries to turn them into its docile instruments, they will be able to achieve very little. To work effectively, even a well-designed administrative system needs the energetic participation of its citizens.

Glossary

Abstinence from evil. Refraining from doing evil, rather than positively doing good. Mill describes Christian morality as negative, rather than positive, and in need of being supplemented from Greek and Roman sources, which place a greater emphasis on public morality and duty. He suggests that Christians' main motive for abstaining from evil is to get to heaven. This fails to do justice to Jesus' teaching as it appears in the Sermon on the Mount.

Accountable (of governments). Responsible to an electorate.

Alliance (United Kingdom Alliance). This was formed in 1853, after the sale of alcohol was banned in the state of Maine, to co-ordinate the efforts of the temperance movement in Britain, and to lobby parliament to ban alcohol. See Maine Law and temperance movement below.

America/United States. Mill uses the example of the United States in *On Liberty*. He criticizes the ban on the sale of alcohol in some American states as an infringement of individual liberty, but expresses admiration of Americans' commitment to freedom, administrative abilities and willingness to participate in government.

Aristocracy. Mill contrasts democracy with aristocracy: government by the best citizens or a dominant class.

Ascendant class. A dominant, ruling or upper class. Mill argues that, in a society with such a class, the prevailing morality will reflect its interests. See also class interests below.

Atheism. Not believing in the existence of God.

Authority. Generally power or right. In *On Liberty*, it also refers to (powers of) government/a system of government that emphasizes order and control in society rather than (and possibly at the expense of) individual liberty.

Barbarians/barbarism. Historically, the term was used to denote either those who were not Greek (and who did not have access to the benefits of Greek civilization), or tribal groups outside the Roman Empire, and who were not Christian. Mill uses it to refer to people who have not attained a high level of education and civilization. He accepts that despotism, as opposed to individual liberty, is an appropriate form of government for people who have not got beyond this stage of development.

Bentham, Jeremy (1748–1831). Utilitarian philosopher, author of the *Principles of Morals and Legislation* and friend of both John Stuart Mill and his father, James Mill.

Blasphemer/blasphemy. Insulting God, or calling God's goodness into question. Mill points out that Jesus was condemned to death for blasphemy.

Breach(es) of the peace. Act which is likely to lead to public disorder, and for which someone can be arrested.

Bureaucracy. Extensive organization of officials, employed by the state to carry out administrative responsibilities, a civil service. Mill points out the dangers of an overlarge government bureaucracy, which recruits a country's most able citizens into its service, in Chapter V of *On Liberty*.

Calvinism. Mill is referring to the teaching of John Calvin (1509–64) and the beliefs of those who follow his teaching.

Calvinism emphasizes God's sovereignty and predestination: the idea that God predetermines the salvation or damnation of human beings.

Central (of administration, government). National government, a government of a whole country as opposed to local government.

China. Mill uses China (and the East generally) as an example of the dangers of discouraging individuality and creating an overlarge bureaucracy: progress and change become difficult, if not impossible, to achieve.

Christianity/Christians. Mill is critical of Christian morality, and also of contemporary Christians, who pay lip-service to Jesus' teachings, but fail to base their lives on them. See abstinence from evil above.

Christian morality/ethic. See Christians/Christianity and abstinence from evil above.

Civil or social liberty. This is the subject of *On Liberty*: where the boundary is to be drawn between individual liberty and society's legitimate interference with individual conduct. Mill argues that society is only entitled to interfere to prevent harm to the interests of others.

Civil service. Body of officials, employed by the state, to carry out administrative responsibilities. In Chapter V of *On Liberty*, Mill discusses reforms, proposed in the Northcote–Trevelyan Report (1854), to introduce competitive examinations for civil service recruitment. These were introduced by Gladstone's Liberal government in 1870. See also bureaucracy above.

Class interests. What is of advantage to a particular class or section of society. Mill argues that society's morality often reflects the interests of its ruling class. See also ascendant class above.

Collective opinion. The general view of society on a particular issue.

Competitive examination. An examination to select applicants for a place or post on merit, by testing their ability and/or aptitude. See also civil service above.

Comte, Auguste (1798–1857). French thinker and writer, founder of positivism and inventor of the term 'sociology', and author of *The System of Positive Polity*.

Conscience(s). Human beings' awareness of what is right and wrong, which deters them from contemplating or committing wrong actions.

Consent. In *On Liberty*, it refers to the consent or agreement of a representative body or parliament being necessary before a government introduces a law or takes action.

Constitution/constitutional. A statement (generally written) of the basic principles by which a country is governed, providing (usually) for a democratic or representative element. Mill refers to 'constitutional countries', by which he means states with a constitution and some form of representative government (but not necessarily a fully democratic one), and therefore some recognition of individual rights, as opposed to one governed by an absolute monarch or ruler.

Constitutional checks. Provision in the constitution requiring a government to receive the approval of, or at least to consult, a representative body before it introduces a law or takes action.

Contract (social). The idea that the mutual responsibilities and obligations of members of society are based on a contract, which may or may not be regarded as an historical event.

Custom. That which is usually done, the usual practice. In *On Liberty*, Mill urges his readers not to be ruled by custom. Unless the customary way of doing things is challenged, human beings will not develop to their full potential, and political and social reform will not take place.

Czar. Title of the emperors of Russia.

De Tocqueville, Alexis-Charles-Henri Clerel (1805–59). French writer and historian, enthusiastic advocate of democracy and freedom, and author of *Democracy in America* and *The Old Regime and the Revolution*.

Degenerate. Decayed, weakened.

Democracy. Government by the people, or one that is chosen by, and accountable to, the people.

Democratic constitution. A constitution which provides for government by the people, or for a government that is chosen by, and accountable to, the people. See constitution above.

Derby, Earl of. See Stanley below.

Despotism. Government by an absolute ruler or tyrant, with no representative element and usually little or no recognition of the rights of individual citizens.

Disraeli, Benjamin (1804–81), Earl of Beaconsfield (1876). Conservative politician and writer, whose novels include *Coningsby* and *Sybil*. Chancellor of the exchequer under the Earl of Derby, 1852, 1858 and 1866–8, prime minister, February–December 1868, and 1874–80.

Dissemination/disseminate (of power and information). Mill refers to the 'dissemination of power' by central government, by which he means that governments should devolve administrative powers to local authorities, such as municipal (city or town) councils. He also argues that, in order to ensure efficient local government, central government should collect information about good administrative practice from a wide range of sources, and disseminate (circulate) it to local authorities.

Discipline. Mill contrasts the emphasis that some politicians and political parties place on liberty and the rights of the individual with the emphasis others place on discipline in society and the need for society to control some of its members in the interests of others. He argues that both points of view need to be freely expressed if they are to be understood and given due consideration.

Doctrine. What is taught; more generally, as in *On Liberty*, belief or tenet.

Dogma. Belief accepted on authority, and which may be held despite there being a lack of supporting evidence or even evidence that it is not true.

East (the). See China above.

Education. Mill expresses reservations about the extension of education because, by giving people access to the same stock of facts and ideas, it tends to diminish individuality. He is opposed to state education, because he believes that it will become a government device for moulding people to be exactly the same. The role of the state should be confined to requiring parents to ensure that their children receive an education, and operating a system of examinations, to measure their progress. The examinations should test only facts, to prevent the state using them to influence children's opinions.

Elected government(s). Representative government, but not necessarily chosen on the basis of a universal franchise. In nineteenth-century Britain, the right to vote was limited, although the reform acts of 1832, 1867 and 1884 extended it. Women were not allowed to vote at all until 1918, and women below 30 were not able to vote until 1928.

Elementary Education Act, 1870. This created school boards, with powers to establish elementary schools, in areas where there were insufficient voluntary schools to meet educational needs. The boards were given powers to make bye-laws requiring school attendance. Further Elementary Education Acts of 1876 and 1880 made it the parents' duty to ensure their children received adequate basic education and made it harder for children to gain exemption from school attendance

Engines of moral repression. Public opinion, which is opposed to certain views or actions, and which prevents people expressing the views, or performing the actions, even though the actions affect only themselves.

England. Mill refers to 'England', but this seems to include Britain/United Kingdom as a whole. For the most part, he uses examples from Britain to illustrate and support his arguments.

Equality. Mill refers to political groups which wish to defend existing property rights and those which wish to achieve more equality in this area.

Ethical matters. Moral questions.

Europe. Mill believes Europe's remarkable progress in such areas as politics and education has been due to its social and cultural diversity. However, he believes that, even in Europe, change is only embraced if everyone accepts it, while individuality, which helps to promote new ideas and experiments in how to live, is discouraged.

European liberalism. Mill is referring to the nineteenth-century movements in Europe, which sought to overthrow, or introduce democratic elements into, despotic regimes. Mill accuses them of having a rather naive view of the nature of democratic government. Representative governments might also abuse their powers, and so, even in democracies, minority and individual liberties would need to be safeguarded.

External control. Control of individual behaviour by others/ society. Mill believes that this should only be permitted where individual conduct affects the interests of others.

Fermented drink(s). Alcohol.

Fornication. Casual sexual relations.

Fox-hunting. A ban on fox and deer-hunting and hare-coursing came into effect in England and Wales in February 2005. Hunting with dogs was banned in Scotland in 2002.

Free trade. This was one of the major political issues in the first half of the nineteenth century in Britain. Traditionally, British governments had regulated trade, and protected home producers, through duties on imports. Duties on some goods were cut in the 1820s, but those on corn kept its price high. In 1846, the prime minister, Robert Peel, responding to extensive campaigning, repealed the Corn Laws, and by the 1860s Britain was a free trade country.

Freedom of conscience. The right to hold whatever opinions we choose, and to express them freely.

Future life. Life after death.

Gambling-house. Casino.

Genius(es). Person of outstanding intellectual ability, capable of creative and original thought. Mill is more concerned with those whose genius relates to new political or moral theories, or imaginative experiments in living, than genius in such fields as art or music. He argues that society does not value such genius, which requires an atmosphere of freedom, not generally available in nineteenth-century society, in order to flourish.

Gladstone, William Ewart (1809–98). Originally a Conservative politician, who became the leader of the Liberal Party. He was president of the board of trade and secretary for war and colonies under Peel, chancellor of the exchequer under Aberdeen, Palmerston and Russell and prime minister from 1868–74, 1880–5, February–August 1886 and 1892–4. His first ministry passed the Elementary Education Act, 1870, introduced the secret ballot (Ballot Act, 1872), reorganized the legal system (Judicature Act, 1873), reformed the army, and brought in competitive examinations for the civil service.

Homosexuality. Following the 1957 Wolfenden Report, the law relating to homosexuality was eventually reformed by the Sexual Offences Act, 1967.

Hope of heaven and the threat of hell. Mill argues that the main purpose of (following) Christian morality is to secure a place in heaven after death, and to avoid being sent to hell. See also Christianity/Christians and abstinence from evil above.

Idea of abstract right. Mill does not base his argument for individual freedom on an abstract theory about what human rights are, but on utilitarian principles, which reflect human interests and needs. According to Mill, humans are progressive beings, who need individual freedom, in order to develop their full potential. See also individuality and the ultimate appeal in ethical matters is utility below.

Individual independence. What the individual is allowed to do without interference from others.

Individuality. Mill wishes to see people achieving the fullest development of their individual powers, and learning how to think for themselves, for which freedom of thought and action (except where it impinges on other people) is essential. He believes that cultivation of individuality will produce worthwhile new ideas and interesting experiments in ways of living, which will challenge, and possibly replace, existing ones.

Infallible/infallibility. Incapable of making a mistake. Mill argues that those who wish to suppress an opinion are not infallible; they simply confuse their certainty with absolute certainty.

Intemperance. In *On Liberty*, excessive drinking of alcohol.

Jesus. Founder of Christianity. Mill uses the example of Jesus to illustrate the dangers of trying to suppress people's views because they differ from our own. Jesus was regarded as the very opposite of what he was, and condemned as a blasphemer. Mill criticizes the way that contemporary Christians claim to follow Jesus, but do not conduct their lives by his teachings. He also maintains that Jesus' teaching, as recorded in the New Testament, does not contain (because he did not intend it to) all the essential elements of the highest morality. See also blasphemer/blasphemy and Christianity/Christians above and supreme goodness below.

Johnson, Dr Samuel (1709–84). Writer, literary critic and lexicographer, who enjoyed enormous influence in the literary world in the eighteenth century. Author of *A Dictionary of the English Language*, *Rasselas* and the collections of essays, *The Rambler* and *The Idler*.

Jury trial. In Britain, trial where the decision about guilt or innocence is made by 12 members of the public, rather than judges or legal experts. Mill holds that being a jury member helps to train people in the responsibilities of citizenship.

Legislature. A state's law-making body or parliament.

Liberty of the will. Free will. Mill explains, at the beginning of *On Liberty*, that it is concerned with civil and social liberty, not the question of whether or not human beings have free will. See also civil or social liberty above.

Liberty of thought. The freedom to think what we wish, and to hold whatever opinions we choose, which includes (Mill argues) freedom to express and publish them.

Maine Law. This was passed in 1851, and banned the sale of alcohol unless for a very limited range of purposes. The example inspired temperance movements in other states in America and in Britain. See also Alliance above and temperance movement below.

Marcus Aurelius (121–80 AD). Roman Emperor from 161 to 180, Marcus Aurelius spent most of his reign fighting Rome's enemies. He wrote his *Meditations* during his campaigns.

Mass opinion. See public opinion and tyranny of the majority below.

Maxim(s). Principle, rule.

Mill, James (1773–1836). Father of John Stuart Mill, and utilitarian philospher who worked for the East India Company and wrote a history of British India.

Moderns. In *On Liberty*, this refers to modern Christians, who have developed and modified Christian moral teaching.

Morality. System of moral principles (principles concerning) what is right and what is wrong.

Mormonism. The Church of Jesus Christ of the Latter Day Saints was started by Joseph Smith in the 1830s, and established its base in Salt Lake City, Utah. Its teachings and interpretation of the Bible caused outrage, as did its practice of polygamy (now illegal under Utah law). Mill applies his principle of individual liberty to the Mormons. While it is legitimate to speak out against their beliefs and activities, and to have nothing to do with them, it is not legitimate to try and stop them, provided that all those involved are participating voluntarily.

Municipal institutions. Municipal (city or town) councils. Mill argues that serving on these helps to provide training in citizenship. Local government had been reformed by the Municipal Corporation Act, 1835, which provided for election of councillors by ratepayers. County councils were not created until the Local Government Act, 1888.

New Testament. Mill argues that Jesus' teaching in the New Testament does not provide a complete moral system, but criticizes contemporary Christians for not following Jesus' teachings in their own lives. See also Christianity/Christians and abstinence from evil above and Old Testament below.

Newspapers. Mill regrets the fact that so many people allow the newspapers to do their thinking for them, instead of thinking for themselves.

Old Testament. One of Mill's reasons for claiming that the New Testament does not provide a complete moral system is that one of Jesus' concerns was to correct, not replace, Old Testament moral teaching. See also Christianity/Christians, abstinence from evil and New Testament above.

Originality. See genius above.

Orthodox. Generally accepted. In *On Liberty*, it refers to mainstream Christians.

Parties (political). Mill argues that, in the practical concerns of life, truth is found through reconciling opposites, and this is done through a struggle between people of opposing views. Therefore, in politics, different political parties are necessary, to represent the different views, interests and political aims that exist in society (in Mill's day, these were the Conservative and Liberal Parties), and these must be able to campaign freely for their policies.

Partisan. One who is strongly committed to a particular point of view or cause.

Patriot(s). One who is committed to, and always prepared to defend, his country.

Paul, Saint (believed to have died 64–8 AD). Christian missionary and theologian, who, after his conversion to Christianity, dedicated his life to preaching Christianity to the Gentiles (non-Jews). Paul's letters or epistles to the Christian churches form part of the New Testament.

Philanthropic. Motivated by a love of other people and a desire to help them.

Philosopher(s). One who studies and practises/teaches philosophy, the study of ultimate reality, what really exists, the most general principles of things.

Pimp. One who lives on the earnings of prostitutes.

Platonic and Christian ideals of self-government. Mill warns that too much emphasis on self-control, at the expense of the cultivation of individuality, prevents human beings from achieving their full potential.

Political morality. The moral principles or rules which govern political life, policies and decisions.

Political oppression. Being victimized or persecuted by a government or political party for opposing it, or for holding beliefs of which it disapproves. See also social tyranny below.

Political rights. Such rights as free expression, the right to vote and the right to stand for election to a legislature or parliament.

Polygamy. The practice, based on religious belief or cultural tradition, of having more than one wife (or husband) at the same time.

Poor Law Board. Created in 1847, to replace the Poor Law Commission, it supervised relief of poverty, which, under the Poor Law Amendment Act, 1834, was administered locally by boards of guardians, based on unions of parishes.

Poor Rate. The rate levied at parish level to pay for the poor.

Popular constitution (of the legislature). A legislature whose membership is composed of, or includes, representatives chosen by the people.

Precept. Maxim or rule prescribing/guiding conduct.

Press freedom. Freedom of newspapers and journals to publish reports and articles without requiring government approval, no government censorship of the press.

Principle of liberty/individual liberty. Mill's 'very simple principle', to regulate society's relations with individuals. The only purpose for which society can rightfully exercise power over one of its members, against his will, is to prevent harm to others. His own good, whether physical or moral, is not sufficient justification. In conduct affecting only himself, the individual is entitled to absolute independence; he is only accountable to society for conduct which affects others.

Propriety. What is considered proper, acceptable or suitable in conduct or morality.

Protestant(s). Christians who 'protested' against the Roman Catholic Church; those who are members of Christian churches established after the Reformation. See Reformation below.

Public examinations. See education above.

Public opinion. The prevailing view in society on a particular subject. See also social tyranny below.

Pursuit of good. Mill claims that Christian morality is more concerned with showing people how to avoid evil and being condemned to hell than with active pursuit of what is good. See also abstinence from evil above

Rational. Showing evidence of reason, sensible, not extreme.

Reform Act, 1867. This was passed by the Conservatives under the (fourteenth) Earl of Derby and Benjamin Disraeli. It redistributed parliamentary seats on the basis of population, and increased the electorate from just over one million to almost two million.

Reformation. The period, during the sixteenth century, when the protests of Martin Luther (1483–1546) Huldreich Zwingli (1484–1531) and John Calvin (1509–64), in Germany, Switzerland and France, against the theology and practices of the Roman Catholic Church, led to the establishment of Protestant Churches in Europe. Mill maintains that the Reformation, by breaking the authority of the Roman Catholic Church, and removing restrictions on thought and discussion about religion and intellectual matters generally, made progress in these areas possible.

Religious creed. Statement of the main beliefs of a religion.

Religious persecution(s). Being discriminated against or hounded because of religious beliefs or allegiance. Mill warns that the idea it is the duty of one person or group to ensure that another person or group is religious (or signs up to a particular set of religious beliefs) is at the root of all religious persecution.

Representative body. A legislature or parliament with members who are (at least to an extent) elected.

Roman Catholic Church. Mill makes the point that those who opposed and criticized the Roman Catholic Church in the sixteenth century and subsequently were equally as intolerant of religious differences and equally determined to make people accept their teachings, and follow their practices. Toleration (he argues) is only possible in a society in which the different religious denominations realize that no one of them is going to predominate, while full religious freedom is only achieved when religion itself has become a matter of indifference.

Roman Empire. Mill suggests that Christianity only ultimately prevailed in the Roman Empire, because its persecution of Christians was intermittent. He believes that, in general, persecution will always triumph, unless those being persecuted are too powerful to be overcome.

Rousseau, Jean-Jacques (1712–78). Swiss philosopher and author of *Émile, or Education* and *The Social Contract*.

Sabbatarian(ism). The view, which derives from biblical teaching, that Sunday should be set aside as a day of rest, on which certain activities, including work, do not take place. Mill acknowledges the benefits of everybody having the same day of leisure each week, but regards any attempts to force people to observe it as unjustified interference with individual liberty.

School disputations. System of teaching and examination, used in medieval universities and schools, which required students and pupils to defend a particular position in debate.

Sect. Religious denomination, or group of people who share the same (religious) beliefs that differ from the generally accepted ones.

Self-abnegation. Self-denial.

Self-government. In *On Liberty*, this refers to a government chosen by, and responsible to, the people.

Self-regarding (matters). Beliefs and actions which affect only the individual, and with which society is not entitled to interfere, even if it disapproves of them.

Sentiments. Feelings, views.

Siberia. Place of exile or punishment for opponents of the Russian (and later Soviet) government.

Singularity. (Extreme) individuality.

Social rights. Rights that people have as members of society.

Social tyranny. Public opinion, directed against minorities or individuals, whose beliefs or way of life society regards as unacceptable or unorthodox. Mill believes that adverse public opinion can be harder for minorities or individuals to endure than political oppression. See political oppression above.

Socrates (c. 470–399 BC). Greek philosopher, who features in the works of Plato. He devoted his life to the pursuit of philosophical truth, but was executed for questioning the existence of the gods recognized by the Athenian state.

Socratic dialectics. The technique employed by Socrates (as he appears in Plato's *Dialogues*) of teaching through a series of questions, which leads the student to grasp the truth.

Stanley, Edward George, fourteenth Earl of Derby (1799–1869). Whig, later Conservative politician. Chief secretary for Ireland and secretary for war and colonies under Earl Grey, secretary for war and colonies under Peel, prime minister, February–December 1852, 1858–9, 1866–8.

Stanley, Edward Henry, fifteenth Earl of Derby (1826–93). Originally a Conservative MP, he was twice foreign secretary under his father (the fourteenth Earl of Derby) and Disraeli, but later joined the Liberal Party and was colonial secretary under Gladstone. This is the Stanley referred to in *On Liberty*.

State education. Education provided by the state. See also education above.

Supreme goodness. The highest level of goodness. Mill argues that Christian morality, due to insufficient emphasis on public obligation and our duty to others, does not provide a complete guide to life and, unless supplemented from Greek and Roman sources (which do), produces people who are too submissive to God's will, and too concerned about an afterlife, to reach the highest levels of goodness in this one.

Temperance movement. The movement to ban, or at least limit, the sale of alcohol. It resulted in the banning of the sale of alcohol (and ultimately Prohibition) in the United States and to licensing acts, regulating sales of alcohol, in Britain. See Maine Law above.

The ultimate appeal in ethical matters is utility. Mill sets out his version of utilitarianism in his *Utilitarianism*. The basic idea of utilitarianism is that actions are right to the extent that they promote pleasure and the (greatest) happiness, and wrong to the extent that they promote pain.

Theologian(s). One who studies and practises/teaches theology, the academic discipline concerned with the study of religion/religious beliefs and teachings.

Theological. Religious, concerned with God.

Toleration (religious). When different religions/religious groups are allowed (or allow each other) to co-exist without discrimination or persecution. This was not achieved in Britain until the nineteenth century. Although there was little active discrimination against Nonconformists during the eighteeenth century, the seventeenth-century Corporation and Test Acts, designed to exclude non-Anglicans from municipal and government office, were not repealed until 1828 and the Catholic Emancipation Act was not passed until 1829. Mill makes the point that genuinely religious people always have reservations about toleration, and that full religious freedom (which would include the absence of hostile public opinion, as well the absence of legal penalties) is only found in societies where religion is a matter of indifference.

Tyranny of the majority. The tyranny that the majority in society can exercise over minorities or individuals who dissent from generally held views, or who do not conform to generally accepted modes of conduct. See also social tyranny above.

Virtuous life. A life characterized by adherence to high moral standards.

Voluntary associations. Voluntary societies or groups, formed for such purposes as mutual help or charity, and which do not owe their existence to, or receive support from, the state. Mill is keen to ensure the existence of as many organizations as possible (charities, privately owned businesses and industries, as well as independent local authorities and the universities), which are free of central government control. He regards expansion of central government's role as likely to diminish personal freedom and individuality, because it gives the state increasing opportunities to mould its citizens' attitudes and to make them more dependent upon (and therefore subservient to) it. At the same time, institutions and organizations, which are free of government control, give people valuable opportunities for citizenship training, and equip them to put the state's activities under critical scrutiny.

Von Humboldt, Baron Wilhelm (1767–1835). Prussian diplomat, philosopher, linguist and author of *On the Limits of State Action*.

The Briefly Series